MW00987639

JAMES W.
MOORE

If God Has
a Refrigerator, Your
Picture Is on It

DIMENSIONS
FOR LIVING
NASHVILLE

IF GOD HAS A REFRIGERATOR, YOUR PICTURE IS ON IT

This book is printed on acid-free, elemental-chlorine–free paper.

Library of Congress Cataloging-in-Publication Data

Moore, James W. (James Wendell), 1938–
  If God has a refrigerator, your picture is on it / James W. Moore.
    p. cm.
  ISBN 0-687-02681-4 (pbk.: alk. paper)
  1. Christian life—Methodist authors.   I. Title.
  BV4501. 3 .M663 2003
  231. 7—dc21   2002015888

Scripture quotations, unless otherwise noted, are from the New Revised Standard Version of the Bible, copyright © 1989, by the Division of Christian Education of the National Council of the Churches of Christ in the United States of America. Used by permission.

Scripture quotations noted KJV are from the King James or Authorized Version of the Bible.

Scripture quotations marked RSV are taken from the Revised Standard Version of the Bible, copyright 1946, 1952, 1971 by the Division of Christian Education of the National Council of the Churches of Christ in the United States of America. Used by permission. All rights reserved.

Scripture quotations marked Phillips are taken from *The New Testament in Modern English*, translated by J. B. Phillips and published by The MacMillan Company. Copyright © J. B. Phillips, 1958.

If God Has a Refrigerator, Your Picture Is on It, title adapted from text in *A Gentle Thunder,* copyrighted material, W. Publishing, 1995, Max Lucado, page 122. Used by permission.

03 04 05 06 07 08 09 10 11 12 — 10 9 8 7 6 5 4 3 2 1

MANUFACTURED IN THE UNITED STATES OF AMERICA

*For Sarah,
Paul, Dawson,
and Daniel*

CONTENTS

INTRODUCTION

If God Has a Refrigerator, Your Picture Is on It

Scripture: 1 John 4:7-12; Luke 15:11-32

His name was Kurt. He was the stocker at the local supermarket. He was hard at work back in the stockroom, when he heard the sound of a new voice on the supermarket P.A. system. The delicate voice was calling for a carryout at register number four. Kurt was almost finished in the stockroom and was ready for some fresh air, so he responded to the call. As he approached the checkout stand, a gorgeous smile caught his eye. The new employee behind the register was a stunningly beautiful young woman. Their eyes met, and Kurt fell head over heels in love!

At the end of the day, Kurt waited by the punch clock to get another look at her. After she punched out, he looked at her card and discovered that her name was Brenda. As Kurt left the store, he saw her walking up the road. Now, he knew three things about her: her name was Brenda, she didn't have a car, and he desperately wanted to take her out.

The next day, he waited outside as Brenda left the supermarket and offered her a ride home. He looked harmless enough, so she accepted. When he dropped her off, he asked if he might take her out to dinner and a movie sometime. She said that that would not be possible. He pressed, and she explained that she would like to go out with him, but she couldn't because she had two children and couldn't afford a babysitter.

Kurt offered to pay for the babysitter, and finally she agreed to go out with him the following Saturday night. But when he arrived at her front door on Saturday night, she had a sad expression on her face. She said she wouldn't be able to go because the babysitter had just called and canceled. To which Kurt replied, "Well, let's just take the kids with us. I'll help you with them. I'm pretty good with kids!"

She tried to explain that taking the children was not an option, but again, not taking no for an answer, Kurt asked if he could meet the children. Finally, Brenda brought him inside. She had a little girl, just as cute as she could be. Then Brenda brought out her son in a wheelchair. He had been born a paraplegic with Down syndrome. Kurt said, "Your children are great! Let's take them with us."

Brenda was absolutely amazed. Most men in Kurt's position would have run away from a woman with two children, especially if one of them had disabilities. That evening, Kurt and Brenda loaded up the children and went to dinner and a movie. Kurt *was* great with the children. When her son needed anything, Kurt would take care of him. Both of the children loved Kurt, and at the end of the evening, Brenda knew that she wanted to marry this man and spend the rest of her life with him. A year later they were married, and Kurt adopted both of her children. Since then, they have added two more children of their own.

Now, you may be wondering what happened to Kurt and Brenda. I mean, how in the world could they support themselves and four children on a supermarket stocker's salary? Well, fortunately, Kurt got another job offer. The family had to move to St. Louis in order for him to take this job, but it was worth the move, because he did get a better salary. You see, Kurt's full name is Kurt Warner; he became a professional quarterback for the St. Louis Rams!

Now, the question that explodes out of this story is this: Where did Kurt Warner learn to love sacrificially and graciously like that? You know the answer, don't you? He learned it from the church. He learned it from the Scriptures. He learned it from God.

Recently, I was speaking at a church campground. A young man there was wearing a T-shirt. The T-shirt was bright yellow, and on the front of it were printed these words: *If God Has a Refrigerator, Your Picture Is on It!* I went over to the young man and said, "I like your T-shirt!"

His face lit up with a big smile, and he said, "Do you know what it means?"

"Well," I said, "my hunch would be that it means that God loves us the way parents love their children; that God is not some angry, vengeful deity, demanding his pound of flesh; that God is not some impersonal computer who rewards us when we do good and punishes us when we do bad; but rather, that God is like that father in the prodigal son parable (Luke 15:11-32), who excitedly runs down the road to meet us, to love us, to forgive us, to redeem us, to celebrate us, to hug us, and to welcome us into the circle of his gracious love."

And the young man in front of me looked down at his T-shirt, smiled, and said, "Cool!"

Our refrigerator at home is covered with pictures of our children and grandchildren. Every time we go to the refrigerator (and I go there a lot!), there they are—those beautiful, magnetized, visible reminders of how much we love our children and grandchildren, and how incredibly precious they are to us. The Scriptures tell us that God loves *us* like that—and *then* some!

It is crucial to note that when Jesus decided to give us the best picture he could think of to describe God, he said that God is like a loving parent—a devoted, caring, compassionate parent who loves us unconditionally, who forgives us unreservedly, who celebrates us unashamedly. Now, I know that, sadly, some parents aren't like that. Sadly, some parents don't do those things. But, Jesus told the parable of the prodigal son to show us what God is like, to show us dramatically and graphically that God is like a devoted, caring parent who loves us unconditionally, who forgives us unreservedly, and who celebrates us unashamedly.

Let's look together at these three wonderful qualities of our gracious God, who, if he has a refrigerator, has on it your picture and mine.

FIRST OF ALL, GOD LOVES US UNCONDITIONALLY

The key to finding the truth of a parable is to look for the surprise in it. The surprise for the listeners who first heard Jesus tell the story in Luke 15:11-32 was the unconditional love of the father. As Jesus would come to the part of the story that describes the prodigal's homecoming, the first-century audience would fully expect the father either to reject the prodigal son altogether or, at best, to put strong conditions on the son's return to the family. Listeners expected the father to say, "I don't know you! You are dead to me! You are not a part of this family anymore!" or at least to say, "Well, you can come back on probation," or "You can be one of my hired hands, but not my son, until you have met certain conditions." Even the prodigal son *himself* expected to hear that! Remember his confession: "Father, I am no longer worthy to be called your son; treat me like one of your hired hands."

You can just picture in your mind the image of those first-century listeners, rubbing their hands together and saying, "Boy, oh boy, is that prodigal son going to get it now! His father is going to rip into him and set him straight!" Imagine their surprise, their disbelief, their shock, when told by Jesus that the father instead ran down the road to meet the prodigal. With his robes flapping in the wind, the father couldn't wait to get to him. He ran to welcome his son home and to *love* him back into the family. Some of those people in that first-century audience may have fainted on the spot! Some of them probably grumbled about this newfangled idea. They were not expecting unconditional love.

Let me tell you about another little boy who got into trouble one day, some years ago. His name was David Leroy. He grew up in a small town near the Sabine River in Louisiana. His father owned the grocery store in that little town and had saved money for years so that he could purchase for the family a brand-new 1928 Buick. It was their prize possession. Even though David Leroy was only eleven years old at the time, he loved to drive the car around in the yard. Of course, since he was only eleven, he never took it out on the road, but he looked for every excuse to drive that 1928 Buick. He would move it from one shady spot to the next in the yard of the old home place.

One morning, David Leroy's mother announced that she needed to take the clothes to the cleaners. "I'll move the car around for you, Mom!" said David Leroy, and before Mom could protest, he was out the door. The car was in the garage. David Leroy was so excited as he rushed to bring the car around to the front for his mother that he forgot to close the driver's side door. And as he backed out, the open door smacked against the garage's entryway. The car door ripped completely off, and with a sickening thud, it fell to the ground! Can you imagine? David Leroy had knocked the door off of the family's brand-new 1928 Buick! His mother was—how shall I put this?—*not* happy! "Look what you've done, young man! You just wait 'til your father gets home. He is so proud of that car, and you've *ruined* it. I'll intercede for you the best I can, but I don't know what in the world your father is going to say or do about this!"

David Leroy's father arrived home just in time for supper. David Leroy chose not to eat that night. Somehow, he wasn't hungry at all! Rather, he stood sheepishly out of sight, just outside the door of the kitchen, and listened to his mother as she told his father what had happened. David Leroy was braced and ready, expecting the worst. But he was surprised by his father's response.

"Well, you're right, Ruby," said Dad. "The car is precious to me, but not as precious as David Leroy. Just as you said, he didn't mean to do it. He was trying to help. We can get the car fixed. The main thing is that no one got hurt. He's our son, and he must feel awful right about now. We just need to love him through this."

You know why David Leroy's father responded like

that, don't you? Because he loved his son unconditionally. Where did he learn to love like that? He learned it from Jesus. By the way, David Leroy survived that mishap and grew up to become one of the great preachers of America, D. L. Dykes! When Dr. Dykes later reminisced about the day he knocked the door off the family's 1928 Buick, he said, "Mom interceded for me, and Dad forgave me; and I learned a lot from them that day about what God is like. I learned from them that day the meaning of *grace,* and it is indeed amazing. I learned from them the meaning of unconditional love."

That's number one: God loves us unconditionally.

SECOND, GOD FORGIVES US UNRESERVEDLY

That's what we see here in the parable of the prodigal son. The father forgives the son freely, graciously, generously, with no reservation. Some time ago, a young woman came to see me. She had done something wrong. She had been living a sordid lifestyle, and she knew it. She admitted it. She described it to me in lurid detail. She was penitent, but haunted. "I've asked God to forgive me, but how can I know I'm forgiven?" she said. "How could God ever forgive me for what I've done?"

I said, "Because Jesus told us that God is like a loving father." She didn't seem convinced, so I said to her, "Imagine that I am your father, and you have just told me all of the things you have done, with all of the shady details. I would have two choices. I could say, 'Get out of my sight. I disown you. I don't ever want to see you again.' Or I could say, 'I'm so sorry this has happened, but I love you with all my heart. Let me help you make a new start with your life.' "

I let that idea sink in, and then I asked, "Which one of those things do you think I would say if you were my daughter?" The young woman replied, "The second one." "Why?" I asked. She said, "Because you are a father, and you love your children." And I said, "Listen! If *I'm* capable of that kind of forgiveness, how much more is our Father God?"

This is what Jesus taught us—that God is like a devoted, caring parent who loves us unconditionally and who forgives us unreservedly.

THIRD AND FINALLY, GOD CELEBRATES US UNASHAMEDLY

Can't you just see that father in the parable, running down the road with this incredible look of joy and relief on his face? He doesn't care what the neighbors will say. All he cares about is that his son was lost and now is found. Reports had come back to the farm that the young man might be dead, and now here he is, home, alive and well.

Some years ago in a small town in West Tennessee, a baby boy was born out of wedlock. As he grew up, life was tough for him. Some children were not allowed to play with him. He was shunned on the playgrounds. People whispered behind his back and called him ugly names. He felt rejected and worthless and lonely. However, on his own, when he got to high school, he started going to church. People were nice to him, but he felt self-conscious, so he stayed in the background.

But then one Sunday morning, as he was leaving the sanctuary, he heard the pastor call his name. He stopped and turned to hear the pastor say those words he had come to dread: "Whose boy *are* you, anyway?" The young man froze in place, felt his whole body tense up, and wished that he could disappear. But then the pastor said, "Hey, I know who you are! I know who you belong to! I can see it now. I see the family resemblance. You are a child of God. I can tell by the way you act that you are close kin to God."

The boy was speechless. The pastor put his big hands on the boy's shoulders and said to him, "Son, you have a great heritage. Now you go out there into the world and claim it." Do you know what that pastor was saying to that boy? He was saying, in effect, "If God has a refrigerator, your picture is on it!"

By the way, that brief incident changed the boy's life. It gave him a new identity, a new sense of worth and purpose. It turned his life around. Because he felt so loved by God, he stopped waiting around for others to love him. He started reaching out to others. Later, he became a great governor of the state of Tennessee, because that day he realized that God loves us unconditionally, forgives us unreservedly, and celebrates us unashamedly (Fred Craddock, *Craddock Stories* [St. Louis: Chalice Press, 2001], pp. 156-57). And he realized that "since God love[s] us so much, we also ought to love one another" (1 John 4:11).

1

Celebrating God's Beautiful Mind

Taking on the Mind of Christ

Scripture: Philippians 2:1-11

Have you seen the movie *A Beautiful Mind?* It is incredible. They didn't give Russell Crowe the Academy Award for his performance in this movie (he won the Best Actor award for *Gladiator* the year before), but they well could have, because his performance is perfect. Jennifer Connelly did win the Best Supporting Actress award for her performance in the film, and it was well earned, because her performance is extraordinary. Ron Howard also won for Best Director and for Best Picture (as one of the producers); these awards were also well earned because he spent ten years studying, developing, and creating this amazing and inspirational project.

A Beautiful Mind was inspired by the true story of a man named John Nash, who is still today one of the world's greatest mathematicians. His discoveries in game theory influence our lives every day, both personally and globally, and the theory won for him a Nobel Prize in 1994. But there is more to the story—much more. I will try to share this with you without giving away the movie for those of you who haven't seen it yet.

John Nash, for all his brilliance, just as he was making a name for himself internationally, became the victim of paranoid schizophrenia. He became delusional, confused, frightened, and extremely paranoid. He started seeing things that weren't really there. One of the most fascinating things about the movie is that as you watch it, you are transported inside the mind of John Nash, and, like him, you can't tell what is real and what is not real. *What is reality, and what is delusion?* That's the painful problem John Nash faces as he descends into madness and then, incredibly, regains the ability to function again. John Nash has been compared to Newton, Mendel, and Darwin, but was also for many years just a man muttering to himself in the corner. His rebirth to normalcy happened in large part because of the unconditional love of his wife, Alicia.

One of the most incredible scenes in the movie occurs when John Nash hits bottom, his darkest hour. He realizes that he is having great difficulty sorting out what is reality and what is delusion. He is sitting on the edge of his bed, depressed, despondent, and confused, agonizing over why he (with his bright mind) can't figure out what is real and what is hallucination.

His wife, Alicia, comes to him. She kneels in front of him. She takes her hand and lovingly touches his face, and says, "John, this is real." She takes his hand and tenderly places it on her face, and says, "This is real." She takes his hand and places it on her heart, and says, "This is real." That moment in the movie is the turning point for John Nash. He begins to get better; and when he wins the Nobel Prize, in his acceptance speech, he says, "All of my life I have sought reality. I looked for reality in mathematics, in physics, in metaphysics, even in the delusional." And then, looking at his wife, he says, "But you taught me the most important lesson in life, that the greatest reality is love."

Now, I'm sure that the title of the movie, *A Beautiful Mind*, refers to the brilliant mind of John Nash. But as I walked away from the movie theater, I found myself thinking that Nash's wife, Alicia, was really the one with the beautiful mind because she was the one who kept on loving him when it was hard to do so. She was the one who practiced unconditional love. She was the one who came close to what the apostle Paul called "the mind of Christ."

Talk about a beautiful mind; there is none more beautiful than the mind of Christ! And our calling as Christians is to take on his Spirit, to take on his personality, to take on his mind. Let me ask you something: Can people see the beautiful mind of Christ in you? Do you resemble and reflect the personality of Jesus? Are you becoming more like the Master each day? Can people see and feel the Spirit of Christ in you?

To bring this closer to home, let me ask you three personal questions. You don't have to share your answers with anyone, but I hope you will grapple earnestly and sincerely with these questions deep in your heart and soul. The three questions flow out of the Scripture for this chapter. In Philippians 2, the apostle Paul gives us one of the greatest descriptions of our Lord, some of the most powerful words in all of the Bible. Look at verse 8. Paul was describing the mind of Christ when he said, "He humbled himself/and became obedient to the point of death—/even death on a cross." In these powerful words, Paul outlines for us three of the most powerful characteristics of our Lord: his humility, his obedience, and his sacrificial love. "He humbled himself/and became obedient to the point of death—/even death on a cross." So the three questions are: (1) Can people see in you Christlike humility? (2) Can people see in you Christlike obedience? (3) Can people see in you Christlike love? Let's look at these together.

FIRST OF ALL, CAN PEOPLE SEE IN YOU CHRISTLIKE HUMILITY?

The son of God humbled himself and took the form of a servant. That is precisely our calling as Christian people, to humble ourselves and take the form of servants. If we could understand that and do that, 99 percent of our problems would be solved. But it's so hard to swallow our pride! It's so hard to check our ego at the door.

Do you know that classic story about the cold-natured turtle, who wanted so badly to go to Florida for the winter? He had a problem: he had no way to get there, no means of transportation. But then, like a flash, a brilliant idea came to him. He had two wild geese friends who were about to fly off to Florida. The turtle got a long piece of stout string, and he persuaded each goose to take an end while he (with his strong jaws) bit down on the string in the middle.

Well, the geese took off with the turtle dangling in the middle, holding onto the string with his mouth. All went well. It was a pleasant flight until they passed over a farmer out in the field. The farmer was impressed—so impressed that he shouted up to them, "What a creative idea! That's wonderful! That's ingenious! Who in the world invented that?" The poor turtle, filled with pride and anxious to take full credit, opened his mouth to say, "I did!" And when he opened his mouth, of course, he let go of the string. And the farmer had turtle soup for supper!

I guess we are all afflicted with that kind of "I" trouble. Remember how the poet put it:

I had a little tea party,
This afternoon at three.
'Twas very small, three guests in all:
I, myself, and me.
Myself ate all the sandwiches,
And I drank all the tea;
'Twas also I that ate the pie and passed the cake to me.

As Mac Davis sang, "It's hard to be humble." But Christ shows us the way to humility. He lived in that spirit, and he taught it. Listen to his words:

"Whoever becomes humble like this child is the greatest in the kingdom of heaven." (Matthew 18:4)
"The greatest among you will be your servant." (Matthew 23:11)
"Blessed are the poor in spirit, for theirs is the kingdom of heaven." (Matthew 5:3)

Let me ask you something: Are *you* becoming more like the Master? Do you have the beautiful mind of Christ? Can people see your Christlike humility?

SECOND, CAN PEOPLE SEE IN YOU CHRISTLIKE OBEDIENCE?

He humbled himself. He became obedient. Can people see in you Christlike obedience? Christlike obedience means following God wherever God leads—even if it is to a cross. Christian obedience means living out the Lord's Prayer—*"Thy will be done."* Christian obedience means standing firm in our faithfulness to God.

How difficult this is! Obedience is hard to come by—especially in today's world. We too quickly are tempted

21

to take the shortcut, the quick fix, the easy way. We too often are like the young man who wrote an enthusiastic love letter to his girlfriend, which read:

> My darling, I love you. My love for you is like a red, red rose that blooms for you alone. It is like the nectar of the heavens. It is my soul's delight. My love for you is so great that I would travel to the ends of the earth for you. I would dare the greatest dangers. I would fight my way to your side though giants should oppose me. Through storm and flood and fire, I would persevere to reach you. Accept this letter as the expression of my undying love.
>
> Yours forever,
> John
>
> P.S. I'll be over to see you Saturday night—if it doesn't rain!

We must see that halfhearted love is out. Halfhearted obedience won't do. It's not enough to *talk* a good game; obedience is *demanded*.

Someone has called it "sanctified stubbornness." Isn't that a great phrase? This kind of Christlike obedience enabled the early disciples to keep on preaching the message of Christ in the face of beatings, ridicule, persecution, imprisonment, and even the threat of death. It is also seen in the faith of John Bunyan. He had been in prison for twelve years. He was offered his freedom if he would promise to stop preaching the message of Christ—to which John Bunyan replied, "I have determined, the Almighty God being my help and shield, yet to suffer—even till the moss shall grow on mine eye-brows rather than thus to violate my faith and principles."

Christian obedience means applying God's will to every situation. It is making Jesus Christ the Lord of every moment. It is regarding every situation, every incident, every occurrence, as a unique opportunity to serve God.

In Alabama, they tell of an interesting incident involving the late Coach Bear Bryant and his Alabama football team. Alabama was playing a very close game with a conference rival opponent. It was the fourth quarter, and Alabama had a very slim lead, when the Alabama quarterback called a risky, razzle-dazzle play. It was a bad call. The play backfired. There was a fumble, and the other team recovered the ball. Only a great defensive effort saved the game for Alabama. Alabama almost lost the game because of the quarterback's risky play.

Now, the quarterback was a sensitive young man, so Coach Bryant didn't say anything to him. He waited until the following Tuesday to correct him. He put his arm around the quarterback's shoulder and said, "Son, I don't believe I would have called that play in the fourth quarter last Saturday. It almost cost us the game." To which the quarterback replied, "Gee, Coach, if I'd had from Saturday to Tuesday to think about it, I wouldn't have called it either!"

The point is that we don't always have "from Saturday to Tuesday" to make up our mind, or to think through our decisions. We Christians, like a quarterback, have to condition ourselves, train ourselves, prepare ourselves to have the presence of mind to obey God in every circumstance, and to apply God's will to every situation.

Now, let me ask you something: Are *you* becoming more like the Master? Can people see in you the beautiful mind of Christ? Can they see in you the spirit of Christlike humility and the spirit of Christlike obedience?

THIRD AND FINALLY, CAN PEOPLE SEE IN YOU CHRISTLIKE LOVE?

"[Christ] humbled himself / and became obedient to the point of death— / even death on a cross." Self-giving, sacrificial love—this was the underlying current of Jesus' entire life. It was the key theme of his teachings and his witness. He is the Master who washes his disciples' feet. He is the Suffering Servant who goes out on a limb for others. He is the Good Shepherd who lays down his life for his sheep. He is the Savior who goes to the cross so that we may live. The life and ministry of Jesus Christ can be summed up in this poignant and powerful phrase: "self-giving, sacrificial love."

That is our calling as Christians—to be self-giving, loving servants. We as Christians are called to live daily in that spirit—called to imitate the sacrificial love of Christ. Let me tell you what I mean.

During the 1992 Los Angeles riots, an amazing act of sacrificial love took place. A Hispanic man named Fidel Lopez had been jerked out of his truck and beaten senseless by the rioters. He was being hit mercilessly with sticks and bats and bottles. He was being kicked repeatedly and battered with angry fists. A crowd of people stood by and watched. Suddenly an African American minister, the Reverend Bennie Newton, came upon the scene. Immediately he ran and dove, covering Fidel Lopez's body with his own. He screamed at the wild-eyed mob, "Stop it! Kill him, and you'll have to kill me too!"

Bennie Newton turned back the rioters, then picked up the unconscious man and drove him to Daniel Freeman Hospital. Later, Pastor Newton took up a collection at his church to repay Fidel Lopez the $3,000 the looters had stolen from him that afternoon. Some days later, the two men met. They hugged each other and cried. Fidel Lopez said to the Reverend Newton, "How can I ever thank you? You saved my life. You could have been killed yourself. But *why*? Why did you do it? Why did you risk it?"

I love Bennie Newton's answer. He said, "I did it simply because I am a Christian. I believe in sowing love, not hate. I believe in helping, not hurting. I believe in Jesus Christ, the Prince of Peace and love. I believe in that One who died on a cross to save us!"

Let me ask you something—can *you* love like that? Are you with each passing day becoming more like the Master? Are you more like him now than you were this time last year? We become like what we love; and the more we love Christ, the more humble, the more obedient, the more loving we will be.

2

Celebrating God's Strength

When We Have to Face the Unknown

Scripture: 1 Samuel 17:1-24, 32-45, 48-49

Calvin, the little boy in the delightful comic strip Bill Watterson used to draw, "Calvin and Hobbes," comes marching into the living room early one morning. His mother is seated there in her favorite chair. She is sipping her morning coffee. She looks up at young Calvin. She is amused and amazed at how he is dressed. Calvin's head is encased in a large space helmet. A cape is draped around his neck, across his shoulders, down his back, and is dragging on the floor. One hand is holding a flashlight, and the other a baseball bat.

"What's up today?" asks his mother.

"Nothing, so far," answers Calvin.

"So far?" she questions.

"Well, you never know," Calvin says. "Something could happen today." Then Calvin marches off, saying, "And if anything does, by golly, I'm going to be ready for it!"

Calvin's mother looks directly at the reading audience, and she says, "I need a suit like that!"

That's the way many of us feel as we step out of bed each morning, especially in this volatile and frantic—and sometimes quite violent—world in which we live. We want a suit like Calvin's, so that we can say along with him, "Whatever may come my way, I'm going to be ready for it! Bring it on!"

Well, I don't have a suit like Calvin's to give you, but I do have three words—three great words that we can carry with us each day. Or, maybe better put, three great words that will carry us. Here they are:

Encouragement—which means to be full of heart;

Endurance—which means to be full of power;

Enthusiasm—which means to be full of God.

When we have to face the unknown, when we have to face an uncertain future, when we have to face obstacles and challenges, when we have to face a giant foe, it helps so much to be full of heart, full of power, and full of God. It helps to carry with us these three great words: encouragement, endurance, enthusiasm.

Those were indeed the special qualities that enabled the young shepherd boy named David to do battle against that fearsome giant called Goliath. Remember the story with me. Goliath, the Philistine giant, looked and sounded invincible. He was so huge that he towered over everybody. He was so strong that most men couldn't even pick up the spear he carried. And he was covered from head to toe with the finest protective armor available in that day. Goliath was reputed to be mean, ruthless, and cruel, and the insulting taunts he screamed at the Israelites added foreboding weight to the reports of his savage and vicious nature. The Israelite soldiers were scared to death of him. No one wanted to face this giant called Goliath.

But then along came little David, the shepherd boy. David was too young to be in the army, but he had come to the front lines to bring food and supplies to his older brothers. When David arrived at the front and heard the brash, haughty taunts of Goliath, he immediately volunteered to battle the giant.

King Saul hesitated at first to send this inexperienced, young shepherd boy out to challenge the mighty giant, but finally the king gave in. David went out to face Goliath, armed only with a slingshot, five smooth stones, and the absolute confidence that God would go with him and see him through.

Brashly, the giant moved forward to make quick work of young David. But David had a surprise for Goliath. While others thought Goliath was too big to hit, David thought he was too big to miss! With his dependable slingshot, young David struck the giant at his most vulnerable spot—right between the eyes; and the giant went down in defeat. When the Philistine army saw their champion cut down by a little shepherd boy, they promptly went into a panic and ran away, full of fear, and the Israelites won the day!

How could that happen? How could David win that battle against all odds? How could young David prevail in what looked like a hopeless situation? How could David turn that apparent defeat into a smashing victory? I'll give you the answer in three words: encouragement, endurance, and enthusiasm. Or in other words, David was full of heart, full of power, and full of God. Those are precisely the special qualities we need as we face the Goliaths of this world. Those are the three great words we need to carry with us—or to carry us—as we live out our days and face our own modern-day Goliaths. Let me show you what I mean.

FIRST OF ALL, THERE IS ENCOURAGEMENT

That means being "full of heart." The word *encourage,* in French, literally means "to put the heart in." To *discourage* is "to tear the heart out." When David arrived at the front lines that day, he quickly realized that the Israelites were so afraid of Goliath that they had lost heart. But David was full of heart, full of courage, full of confidence, because he remembered how God had been with him and how God had helped him in the past. He was full of heart because he knew that God would be with him and God would help him in the future.

Some of the most powerful moments in the Bible are those poignant scenes where we see God putting the heart into people. There is Moses, brooding in the desert when all of a sudden, God appears to him in a burning bush and puts the heart back into him.

There is Zacchaeus, perched in a sycamore tree, a prisoner of his own loneliness, when suddenly Jesus walks over and puts the heart back into him.

There is Mary Magdalene, crying out in grief at the garden tomb, when suddenly the Risen Lord calls her by name and puts the heart back into her.

And here in 1 Samuel is young David, the shepherd boy, walking up to the front lines of the battle and hearing the arrogant taunts of Goliath, and then feeling God put the heart into him, enabling him to do battle with a giant and to prevail. Putting the heart back into people; I don't know of anything more Godlike than that!

Every year in the first week of January, I attend a meeting of the ministers of some of the largest Methodist churches in America. It's an interesting meeting because there is no agenda or schedule; there are no programs, no workshops, no speakers. Twenty of us just sit around a table and talk about what's going on in our lives personally, what's going on in our churches, how we can help one another, and what we can learn from one another. This time together is often very moving, as the ministers become very vulnerable, and they share their joys and their heartaches. Let me give you a case in point. By the way, I have permission to share this true story with you.

Jim, one of our ministers, once told about how proud he was of his son Eric. Eric had just received a promotion with his company, being made regional manager, the youngest person ever to become a manager in the history of the very large company. But there is more to the story. Jim told us through tears about how just four years before, Eric had been on a self-destructive course. He was on drugs and in a lot of trouble. Eric was 6'3" and weighed 300 pounds. When he was in high school, he would go to the parties and ask people to hit him in the face as hard as they could. It became a popular game: "Let's see who can knock the big guy down." One after another, his classmates would slug him, slamming their fists into his face as hard as they could.

Jim said that on many nights, he and his wife would hear a thump at the front door. They would investigate and find that Eric's buddies had brought him home and dumped him onto the front porch, his body full of drugs and his face swollen and bloody, with puffy eyes and with purple bruises all over from the blows he had taken. Obviously, his parents were worried sick about him, and they tried everything, but nothing seemed to reach him.

Finally, Eric ran away from home, and he took a job at a feed store. One day, a man came in to buy some feed for his horses. Eric was impressed with the man's red sports car. He went on and on about it, complimenting that car. "You know, Eric," the man said to him, "you could have a car like this if you'd put your heart and mind to it. I can tell that you are a good worker, and if you ever decide you're ready to get your act together, let me know, and I'll help you." Eric and the man with the red sports car became friends, and the man kept encouraging Eric.

Finally, one day the man offered Eric a job with the company he worked for. Eric took the job, and with the help of that man—and with God's help—Eric's life was turned completely around. He did well in his job. He came back to his family, back to his church, and back to his God. And now, Eric not only has a good managerial position, but he goes everywhere anyone will listen to him to tell his story about how God forgave him, redeemed him, and turned things around for him; and how for him, that man in the red sports car became the agent of God's love and encouragement.

Recently, Jim shared this story in his sermon one Sunday morning. After the service, people came by with the usual responses: "Nice sermon today," "Thanks for your message," "Good words," and so forth. Suddenly, a first-time visitor came by. He shook Jim's hand, and he said, "I'm that man." "Pardon me?" Jim said. "I am that man," said the visitor, "the man with the red sports car. I'm the man who gave Eric his job. I didn't know you were his father. I just happened to drop in this morning."

Jim told us, "I grabbed that man and hugged him with all of my might, and I tried desperately to find the right words to express my gratitude to him for what he had done for my son, and for the encouragement he had given to him." *Encouragement*—to be full of heart. That's a great spirit and a great word to take with us for the living of these days.

By the way, have you ever noticed in the Scripture how so often when an angel of the Lord appears to someone, the first thing the angel says is, "Don't be afraid! Take heart!" That's the word that God has for us right now. "Take heart": the word of *encouragement*.

SECOND, THERE IS ENDURANCE

This means being full of power. The Greek word for power is *dunamis*. The word *endurance* means to be filled with power, to have power within; and specifically it means "persistence" or "staying power"—the strength to see something through to the end. It's so important to finish what we start! Young David didn't just make a good beginning. He didn't just talk a good game. He finished the job. He saw it through. He completed the task.

You know, four seconds can be a long time. Ask Derrick. Derrick was the senior quarterback of his local high school football team. With only four seconds remaining in the playoff game against their biggest rival, Derrick's team led 20-13 and had the ball, facing fourth down right on the 50-yard line. Derrick had played the best game of his career. Just one more play to make, just four seconds to use up. The coach told Derrick to take the snap, turn, and run toward his own end zone until the clock ran out. If they chased him, he was to run on out of the end zone, giving the other team a safety—two points— which would still ensure a win for their team. However, Derrick got confused. He took the snap, ran to his end zone, and when he heard the final horn sound, he thought the game was over. So instead of running on out of the end zone, in jubilation he threw the ball up into the air, to celebrate what he thought was a victory for his team.

A defensive back for their rivals, who had chased Derrick for 50 yards, caught the ball in the end zone. The officials' ruling: Derrick's toss into the air was an intercepted pass, the catch by the defender was a touchdown for the other team, and the score was now 20-19. The rules allowed the rival team then to attempt a two-point conversion, following their touchdown; they made it, won the game 21-20, and knocked Derrick's team out of the playoffs. Derrick was heartsick, and all because he stopped too soon. If he had kept on running, the victory would have been his.

There's a message there somewhere, and I think it has to do with endurance, the power to finish what we start. First, there is encouragement—to be full of heart. Second, there is endurance—to be full of staying power.

THIRD AND FINALLY, THERE IS ENTHUSIASM

Enthusiasm literally means being "full of God." That's what enabled young David to do what he did. That's what gave him the courage and confidence to face a giant. David was filled with the Spirit of God. He trusted God. He knew God was with him. He was full of God.

Let me ask you something: How is it with you? Are you full of heart? Are you full of staying power? Are you full of God?

Some years ago, a woman was cleaning her parakeet's birdcage when she accidentally sucked her pet parakeet, Chippie, into her vacuum cleaner. Horrified at what she had done, she frantically ripped open the vacuum bag. She found Chippie in there, stunned and shaken, but still alive. Chippie was covered with dust and dirt, so the woman grabbed him and ran to the sink, turned on the faucet, and held him under the cold water to clean him off. Then she ran with Chippie to the bathroom, turned on the hair dryer, and held him in front of the blast of hot air to dry him off. It was (to say the least) a traumatic morning for Chippie the parakeet. Later, someone asked the woman, "How's Chippie doing now?" She answered, "Well, Chippie doesn't sing much anymore. He just sits and stares."

Lots of people today are like Chippie. They have been knocked around by life so much that they don't "sing" much anymore. They just sit and stare. Put that over against this next story.

Her name was Myra. She was in her eighties and was one of the finest human beings I had ever known, always radiantly happy, always cheerful, always grateful, always hopeful, always positive, always enthusiastic about life. One day I said to her, "Myra, you are always smiling. You light up the room when you walk in. What is it about you? Why are you so confident and happy all the time?" Her answer was simple but eloquent. She said, "Because I am a Christian. I know each day that I have a choice. I can be happy or sad. So, since I'm a Christian, I choose to be happy."

Myra was full of heart, full of staying power, full of God. *Encouragement, endurance, enthusiasm:* three great words to live by.

3

Celebrating God's Urgent Priorities

Do Your Best to Come Before Winter

Scripture: 2 Timothy 4:6-13, 21a

Some years ago, a doctor came to see me one Thursday morning. His face was radiant. I could tell he was excited about something.

"Jim," he said, "I want to tell you something you don't know about me. I'm an alcoholic, and yesterday was a big day for me." He said, "It was my fifteenth anniversary of sobriety. I haven't had a drink now for fifteen years. I feel so good, and things are just going so great for me and my family, and my career. I owe it all to your good friend, Tom. Fifteen years ago," he said, "I was living in Dallas, and Tom was my pastor where we attended church. At the time, my life was an absolute mess. I was addicted to alcohol. I was drinking so heavily that I was about to lose everything. My family, my career, my friendships, and my health were all being destroyed by my drinking problems."

"Then," he said, "I hit bottom. I went to Tom, and he was great. He helped me so much. He got me involved in AA. He helped my family. He brought me back to God. He turned it around for me." He said, "I owe Tom so much, and as soon as we finish our visit, I'm going to get in my car and drive to Dallas, and I'm going to tell

Tom what I've wanted to tell him for fifteen years—how indebted I am to him, how grateful I am to him, how he was so instrumental by the grace of God in turning my life around. For fifteen years I have wanted to say thank you to Tom, and today I am going to do it!"

"Oh, Doctor," I said to him, "you haven't heard. I'm sorry to tell you this, but Tom had a heart attack in a church meeting last week, and he died." I will never forget the look on the doctor's face as he realized that he had waited too long.

But the truth is that we can all relate to that, can't we? We all know the feeling of putting off and putting off, of procrastinating and waiting too long.

How many letters have never been written?

How many phone calls have never been made?

How many compliments have been left unsaid?

How many *I'm sorry*'s remain unspoken?

How many *thank you*'s have never been uttered?

How many *I love you*'s are still unexpressed?

How many commitments are still not made because we waited too long?

Now, this brings us to the Scripture for this chapter in 2 Timothy. Let me put this passage in context. The apostle Paul had known Timothy for some years. Paul was the one who had led Timothy to know Jesus Christ. Paul had known Timothy's mother. Over the years, Paul had trained Timothy in the faith and had taken Timothy along with him on his missionary journeys. It is believed by some that 2 Timothy was one of the last things Paul ever wrote. He wrote it while in prison, not long before being executed by the Romans, and Paul knew when he wrote these words that his days on this earth were numbered.

Paul was in prison in Rome, and Timothy was in Ephesus, so Paul was writing to ask Timothy to come see him as soon as he could, and to bring his cloak (to warm his body), his books (to warm his mind), and his parchments (the Scriptures, to warm his soul). And then Paul wrote this to Timothy: "Do your best to come before winter" (4:21*a*).

Now, the question is, did Timothy come? Did he actually get there before the apostle Paul died? The truth is, we don't know. The Bible never says. Church history doesn't tell. But let me ask you something: Would *you* have gone? If Paul wrote to you and said, "Come, and come quickly. I don't have much time left. I really need to see you before I die. Please come and bring my coat, and my books, and especially my Bible. I need your support and companionship," would you have gone? Or would you have procrastinated?

This phrase, "Come before winter," became the title of one of the most famous sermons ever preached in America. It was preached thirty-seven times from the pulpit of First Presbyterian Church in Pittsburgh, Pennsylvania, by Clarence Edward McCartney, one of the great preachers of the twentieth century. After he preached it the first time, the church members were so moved that they called a special meeting of their church board and mandated that every year, Clarence McCartney would preach that sermon again. They wanted to hear that sermon every year; and for thirty-seven years, every year, Clarence McCartney preached that sermon!

Now, in that sermon, Clarence McCartney painted a powerful image by raising this question: What if Timothy delayed? What if he didn't go immediately? What if he said, "Of course I'll go, but I've got a lot of stuff going on right now. I'll go, but a little later." And then, what if, when he got down to the dock some time later, he was told, "Sorry. It's too late. It's wintertime now. It's too cold. The sea is too rough. Can't go now. Wait 'til after winter." What if, when spring came, Timothy went down to the dock, took the first ship to Rome, and finally arrived there, wondering, "Am I in time?"

Clarence McCartney imagined this amazing scene, where Timothy goes to the prison and says to the jailer, "I'm here to see the apostle Paul." And the jailer says, "You must be Timothy. Haven't you heard? Paul was executed last winter." And then the jailer says, "Timothy, he was looking for you. Every day, every time when I would go to his cell to take him his meal, he would always say, 'Timothy, is that you?' 'Is this Timothy?' 'Has Timothy come?' And when Paul died, the last words he said were, 'Tell Timothy, my beloved son in the faith, that I love him, and I always will, throughout all eternity.' " (Thanks to Tom Tewell for this information, *Keep the Change*, audio series.)

Now, how would you feel if you were Timothy, and you hadn't made it in time? We can all relate to that, can't we? We all know the feeling of putting off and putting off and putting off—until it's too late. But please don't misunderstand me. I'm not trying to lay a heavy guilt trip on you. Rather, I simply want to raise this question for us to grapple with: What is God asking you to do? What is the thing that God is calling you to do right now in your life? What is the step that God is asking you to take?

Let me share three thoughts that will prime the pump of your thinking about this.

FIRST OF ALL, IF YOU NEED TO SAY
"I'M SORRY" TO SOMEONE, DO IT NOW

In the Sermon on the Mount, Jesus said, "When you are offering your gift at the altar, if you remember that your brother or sister has something against you, leave your gift there before the altar and go; first be reconciled to your brother or sister, and then come and offer your gift" (Matthew 5:23-24). You know what Jesus was talking about, don't you? He was talking about the way it is between you and "her," the way it is between you and "him." For instance, you see someone coming toward you, and your first inclination is to look the other way or to cross the street so that you don't have to face him or her. Or perhaps a relationship in your group, in your neighborhood, in your home, in your workplace, has grown cold or distant or hostile or sour; you are working in the same office, living on the same street, sharing part of your life, but the relationship is chilly. It's cold, it's tense, it's strained, and it's heavy.

What are you waiting for? Why don't you fix that? Oh, but you say, "It's not my fault." Of course it's not your *fault*, but as a Christian, it is your *responsibility*. Listen! Broken relationships are just too painful, too stressful, too debilitating, and too destructive. They bring ulcers and headaches and insomnia and loneliness and bitterness. What a way to live? It's *no* way to live!

So if you are at odds with any other person right now, please don't let that broken relationship fester any longer. Don't let it poison your spirit or paralyze your soul. For their sake, for your sake, for God's sake, go and fix it, go and make peace. Go and say, "I'm sorry, and I want things to be right with us." Go, and God will go with you.

SECOND, IF YOU NEED TO SAY "I LOVE YOU" TO SOMEONE, DO IT NOW

Have you heard about the man whose wife suddenly died? They had been married for more than forty years. Two days later, after her funeral, he stood at her gravesite and stared at her coffin. Blinking back the tears, he said, "She was the light of my life. She brought such joy to our home. She did everything for me. She was the perfect wife and companion. I loved her so much; and once, I almost *told* her!" Isn't that sad? Isn't that pitiful? "Once, I almost told her."

One of the most tragic things in the world is to go through life not feeling loved and accepted and respected. But another "quiet tragedy" is to go through life loving someone and yet somehow never getting around to telling them. The point is, some things are so urgent, so vital, so crucial—and life can sometimes be so fragile—that we must not, we dare not, put them off. Listen! If you need to say "I'm sorry" to someone, or if you need to say "I love you" to someone—what are you *waiting* for? Do it *now*!

THIRD, IF YOU NEED TO SAY YES TO GOD, DO IT NOW

Have you heard about the man who was asked, "How are your children doing in school these days?" "Well, they are doing better," he replied. "But I do still go to PTA meetings under an assumed name!" Many parents can relate to that and understand that. And obviously, that father was just kidding! But the truth is, God is the opposite of that. God openly claims us. God openly seeks us out. God openly reaches out to us. God openly, intentionally, graciously, relentlessly, sacrificially offers to us the gift of salvation, the gift of forgiveness, the gift of eternal life, the gift of Christ, and the gift of unconditional love.

But we have to do our part. We have to *accept* the gift. What are we waiting for? Why do we hold back? Why are we hesitant to accept God's gracious gift of himself? Why are we so reluctant to say yes to God?

In the summer of 1984, I was attending the jurisdictional conference in Lubbock, Texas. In one of the early ballots (as was expected), my predecessor at St. Luke's United Methodist Church in Houston, Dr. Walter Underwood, was elected bishop. That election did two things: It provided the denomination with a great new bishop; and it opened up one of the best churches in America for a new pastor to be appointed to serve there. During the recesses and breaks at the jurisdictional conference, I would visit with my pastor friends, and we would talk about "Who is going to follow Walter at St. Luke's?" My friends mentioned a long list of names; mine was not one of them! But then I ran into Bishop Ben Oliphint, and he said to me, "Jim, your name is on the St. Luke's list, and I think there is a good chance that you could end up there."

Some weeks later, word came to me that my name had made it to the short list. About this time, a minister friend of mine who was a seasoned veteran minister in Texas called me one night, and he said, "Jim, it's not my style to give advice, but I've called tonight to give you some. Are you listening to me?"

"Yes, sir," I replied.

"Okay," he said, "Here it is: If they offer you St. Luke's, don't ask to see the parsonage. Don't ask what the salary is. Don't ask anything. Just say yes! Do you hear me, young man?"

"Yes, sir," I said.

"Can you say yes?"

"Yes, sir!"

"Okay. That's all you have to do. Just say yes." And then he hung up.

Now, of course, I did say "yes," and as they say, the rest is history. I have been at St. Luke's now for several years. But you know, I've thought about that older minister's advice a lot, and he was right. And that's the advice I want to pass on to you right now. God is offering you his love. Don't ask any questions. Just say yes! And God is calling you to do something. *You* know what it is—to join the church, to teach a class, to sing in the choir, to work with children or youth, to make a pledge, to join a Bible study, to commit your life to Christ. *You* know what it is.

Well, what are you waiting for? Why are you putting it off? What's the hold-up? Do it now; do it today! Do it this moment! Accept God's call! Accept God's gift of love. Just say yes; come to God before winter.

If you need to say "I'm sorry" to someone; if you need to say "I love you" to someone; if you need to say "yes" to God, don't procrastinate any longer. Don't put it off anymore. Life is too short, too fragile.

Just do it *now*!

4

Celebrating God's Unconditional Love

The Real Test of Faith

Scripture: Matthew 25:31-40

I once saw something that fascinated me. I had walked to the Whataburger just down Westheimer Street to pick up a quick lunch. After I placed my take-out order, I noticed her—a middle-aged woman sitting alone in a booth by the window, eating a hamburger and fries with a large chocolate milk shake. She was unusually large, a muscular, commanding, powerful-looking woman who gave the distinct impression that she could be a drill sergeant at Parris Island or play offensive guard for the Houston Texans.

All of a sudden, she glanced out the window. "Oh my goodness," she said. "Look at those kids!" I looked and saw three small children. They were in their swimsuits, with towels draped over their shoulders. They had evidently been swimming, and now they were trying to get back across Westheimer. The three children were holding hands and they were leaning forward like they were about to run a race. They were watching for an opportunity to dash across the busiest street in the known world! At that moment, it seemed even busier than usual.

Suddenly, the woman barked at me: "You! Watch my food!" And I said what anyone in their right mind would have said at the moment: "Yes, ma'am!" She bolted out of the restaurant, rushed to the children, and signaled them to wait. Then, with the authority of a seasoned and confident traffic cop, she marched out into the middle of Westheimer, held up her powerful arm, and stopped all four lanes of traffic! Then she went back to the children, took them by the hand, and walked them across the street as bewildered, but obedient motorists watched with some amusement and lots of appreciation. When she had escorted the children safely across the busy street, she strode back across and then calmly motioned the traffic back to life. Now, let me ask you something. What was it that gave that woman the courage, the strength, the bravado, the guts to do that? The answer is very simple. It was love. As she returned to her food, which I had been dutifully guarding, I said to her, "That was a nice thing you did." She said: "Well, I love kids, and that was a dangerous situation. They needed help. Somebody needed to do something to help them."

The point is obvious: Love is so powerful that it can even stop the traffic on Westheimer—and that's saying something! As I thought about that special act of love, I realized that this is precisely the kind of concern we are supposed to have for all of God's children!

Christ came into the world to show us how concerned God is, how much God cares, how deeply God loves— and he sends us out into the world so that we may love and care for people in the same self-giving way.

That's what this powerful passage of scripture in Matthew 25 is all about. It shows us dramatically that the real test of faith and the authentic sign of discipleship is found in servant love, sacrificial love, self-giving love, Christlike love, unconditional love.

Those who end up on the right hand of God will be those who gave a sandwich to a hungry man, clothes to a person in need, a cup of water to one who is thirsty, kindness to a stranger, a visit to someone sick or in prison. Just little things, but oh-so-big because Jesus is showing us here that when we do good things to others, we do good things to God.

When Francis of Assisi turned his back on a wealthy, privileged life to serve God in simplicity, he took off his expensive robes, threw them aside, and walked out of the city. Along the way, he saw a man with leprosy on the side of the road. He passed him by. But then he remembered Matthew 25. Francis turned around, went back, and hugged the man. Francis then continued his journey. He took a few steps and then turned back to see the man, but amazingly no one was there. For the rest of his life, he was convinced that the man with leprosy that he had encountered had been Jesus in disguise. He may well have been right, because Jesus makes it clear in Matthew 25 that the best way to hug him is to hug our neighbor with unconditional love. This was radical teaching for Jesus' time, because although the people back then believed in love, theirs was a conditional love. They were more than glad to love those who looked like them, and thought like them, and acted like them, and dressed like them. But they had no love at all for people who were different from them, and certainly not for those who were sick and hungry and naked or in prison. And then along came Jesus with this strange new teaching. "Love all people unconditionally. Love all people with no stipulations. Love all people with no strings attached."

The Greek language has many words for our one word, *love*.

Philia, which gives us our words *philanthropy* and *Philadelphia,* means love between friends, humanitarian love.

Storgé means family love.

Eros, which gives us our word *erotic,* means sensuous love; but more, it represents a bargaining love. "You scratch my back, and I'll scratch yours." "I'll do this for you, if you'll do that for me." Which, if you stop to think about it, is not love at all.

And then there is *agape:* this is the word in the Bible that is always used for *God's* love. It means unconditional love, and it is the real test of Christian faith.

Let me ask you something: Do you love unconditionally? *Do* you? *Can* you? *Will* you? Let me bring this closer to home with three thoughts.

FIRST OF ALL, UNCONDITIONAL LOVE IS THE ANSWER FOR OUR RELATIONSHIPS IN THE FAMILY

Do you believe that? Do you believe it enough to practice it in your home? In the book *How to Speak to Youth,* Ken Davis tells about an experiment he tried as a student in speech class in college. Each student was to teach the class on the subject of his or her choice, but students would be graded on their creativity and their ability to drive home a point in a memorable way. Ken Davis chose "The Law of the Swinging Pendulum" as his topic. He demonstrated in numerous ways how a pendulum never can return to a point higher than the point from which it was released. Because of friction-gravity, when the pendulum returns, it will always fall short of its original release point. Each time the pendulum swings, its arc shortens, until finally it stops and is at rest.

Ken attached a three-foot string to a child's toy top and secured it to the top of the blackboard with a thumbtack. He pulled the top to one side and made a bold mark where he let it go. Each time it swung back, he would make a new mark. In less than a minute it came to a stop, and the markings on the blackboard proved the point: *Each and every time, the arc was smaller.* Then Ken asked the class members how many of them now believed that the "Law of the Swinging Pendulum" was true. Every hand went up, including the teacher's.

Everybody thought Ken was through, but he had a surprise for the class. Hanging from the steel ceiling beams in the middle of the room was a huge pendulum (250 pounds of metal weights tied to four strands of 500-pound test parachute cord). Ken asked the professor to climb up on a table and sit in a chair with the back of his head against the wall. Then Ken brought the 250 pounds of metal up to just in front of the professor's nose, and said, "If the Law of the Pendulum is true, then when I release this mass of metal, it will swing across the room and return short of the release point, so the professor is in no danger at all. You *do* believe the Law of the Pendulum, don't you, Professor?" Weakly, the teacher nodded and whispered, "Yes."

Ken released the pendulum. It made a swishing sound as it arced across the room. At the far end of its swing, it paused momentarily and started back. As it started back, you have never seen a man move so fast in your life. The professor literally dove off of that table like a speeding torpedo, and ran as fast as he could to get away from that swinging pendulum. Ken turned to the class and said, "Well, what do you think? Does the professor believe in the Law of the Pendulum?" The students, on the floor with laughter, unanimously shouted, *"No!"*

That's the way many people are in their families with regard to "unconditional love." They *say* they believe in it, but too often they bail out. Unconditional love sounds good, but they are just not sure it will work. Let me tell you something. Unconditional love is the only thing that *will* work in a family. Don't ever say to a child, for instance, "I love you when you are good" or "I love you when you mind me" or "I love you when you clean up your room" or "I love you when you eat your spinach." Don't put conditions on your love for your child. They see right through that, and deep down they know that real love isn't like that. Real love is unconditional. Real love has no strings attached, no stipulations. What we need to say to our children and to other members of our families is this: "I will always love you. There is nothing you can do that will stop me from loving you. You may do some things that disappoint me, but I will never stop loving you. I will love you, come what may."

I once knew a husband and wife who were always trying to "fix" each other. They were both nice, capable, lovable people. They both had many friends, but each one of them wanted to change the other one. Neither of them could love the other unconditionally. In the counseling room, they would say to each other, "I know I'm not perfect, but other people love me as I am. Why can't you? Why do you have to try to *fix* me? Why can't you just love me as I am?" Their marriage didn't make it because they never found how to love unconditionally.

Unconditional love is the answer for our relationships in the family.

SECOND, UNCONDITIONAL LOVE IS THE
ANSWER FOR OUR RELATIONSHIPS WITH OTHERS

With more than a little imagination, someone has written a scenario about what took place when Jesus taught his disciples the lesson of unconditional love for others. Jesus said: "I give you a new commandment, that you love one another. Just as I have loved you, you also should love one another. By this everyone will know that you are my disciples" (John 13:34-35).

And in the scenario, Simon Peter responded with, "Do we have to write this down?"

And Andrew said, "Will this be on the next test?"

And James said, "Will spelling count?"

And Philip said, "Do we have to know it word for word?"

And Matthew said, "When do we get out of here?"

And John said, "Does this apply to all of us?"

And Judas said, "What does this have to do with real life?"

And Jesus wept!

When will we ever learn? Isn't it amazing, and somewhat distressing, how on page after page of the Gospels, Jesus teaches us to love other people unconditionally, and yet we still have all of these questions about it. We are still not sure that it will work. We are still not sure that it applies to us. We are still not sure Jesus meant what he said. Well, he *showed* us that he meant it—on a cross!

I want to ask you a question. Who won the Super Bowl last year? Most people probably don't remember. Who won the Oscar for best actress last year? Most people probably don't remember. Who won the Heisman Trophy last year? Do you remember the current Miss America's name? Can you name two people who have won a Nobel Prize? How did you do? Except for the trivia experts, none of us remembers the headliners of yesterday very well. How soon we forget! And what we've looked at here are no second-rate achievements. These are the best in their fields. But the applause dies down. The awards tarnish. The achievements are forgotten. The accolades and certifications are buried with their owners.

But here's another quiz. Can you remember three or four people who have believed in you, encouraged you, and stood by you in tough times? I'm sure that you did better on this second quiz, and my hunch is that all of those people you thought of had one thing in common—they loved you unconditionally!

The point is clear: The people who really make a difference are not those with the credentials, but those with the love, those who put love first. That's what Jesus is teaching us in Matthew 25.

Unconditional love is the answer for our relationships—first, with the family, and second, with other people.

THIRD AND FINALLY, UNCONDITIONAL LOVE IS THE ANSWER FOR OUR RELATIONSHIP WITH GOD

A couple of months ago, I went to a local production of *Godspell*. This play has many wonderful moments. One of my favorites is that scene toward the end when Jesus is with his disciples in the Upper Room. He takes a bucket of water, a rag, and a mirror, and he goes to his disciples, each in turn, and washes away their painted-on clown faces. Then he holds the mirror up in front of them so that they can see themselves as they really are, and then he hugs them.

The point is obvious and powerful: We don't have to wear false faces, we don't have to hide our inadequacies, and we don't have to pretend to be something we are not. God loves us and accepts us just as we are! We call that "amazing grace," and we like that from God. And yet sometimes we forget to return the compliment, don't we? We want to put conditions on our love for God.

"God, if you will bless me, then I will love you."

"God, if you will answer my prayer and give me what I want, I will serve you."

"God, if you will swing this business deal my way, I will praise you."

"But God, if you don't do what I want, then I'm out of here."

Put that over against this: Job had practically everything go wrong in his life, and still he said, "Though he slay me, yet will I trust in him" (Job 13:15 KJV). And Jesus in the Garden of Gethsemane, facing crucifixion, prayed, in essence, "Father, I trust you. May your will be done." (See Matthew 26:39.)

What is the "take-home value" here? Simply this: Unconditional love is the answer for our relationships in the family, our relationships with other people, and our relationship with God.

5

Celebrating God's Key to Real Life

If God Is Your Co-pilot, Swap Seats!

Scripture: Matthew 6:25-33

Let me tell you about something I like to do when I'm driving. When I see a bumper sticker, I like to pull up next to the car to see if the message on the bumper sticker fits the driver. Sometimes it clearly does. For example, I saw a bumper sticker the other day that said "Don't Worry, Be Happy!" I pulled alongside the car and saw that a young woman was driving the car. She was smiling, singing along with the loud music on her radio, dancing with her head and shoulders to the beat of the music, and tapping out the rhythm on the steering wheel. She was not worrying; she was being happy.

And then I saw one this week that read "God Bless John Wayne." I pulled up to see a guy wearing a cowboy hat. He seemed so into the John Wayne persona that when we stopped at a traffic light, I fully expected him to roll down his window, point at me and say, "Listen *up,* and listen *good,* pilgrim!"

But then, on the other hand, sometimes the driver and the bumper sticker message just don't seem to go together at all. For instance, recently I saw a very profane, off-color bumper sticker on a very nice and expensive car. I pulled up alongside and was amazed to see that the driver was a stylishly dressed, older woman, probably in her late eighties. It makes you wonder what's happening to our world!

A few weeks ago, I saw a car with a bumper sticker on it that read "Honk if You Love Jesus." So I pulled up alongside and honked and smiled and waved. The driver looked at me angrily and acknowledged my honk with a gesture that I don't think was a Christian sign! In all my study of church history, I don't recall that particular gesture ever being listed in any age as a sign and symbol of the Christian faith. That gesture and that message just don't go together. There is something wrong with that picture. So, you never know whether the bumper sticker message really reflects the lifestyle of the driver.

However, I saw a new one the other day that I really like. It read "If God Is Your Co-pilot, Swap Seats." I never could catch up with that car to see whether the driver fit the message. But I do like that message: If God is your co-pilot, swap seats. Now, what I think that means is something that we all need to hear, namely this: Don't just take God along for the ride. Rather, let him do the driving! Put God in the driver's seat of your life. Don't make him your assistant. Let God be the chief pilot in your life's journey.

Some months ago, I pulled into a service station here in southwest Houston to get some gas. I met a young man there who recognized me. He told me that he really enjoyed our church service on television. I invited him to come join us, saying that we would welcome him with open arms. He responded by saying that he is not ready just yet to make that kind of commitment. He said that he was still "enjoying life," and having a great time sowing his wild oats. He indicated that he did believe in God, and that maybe he would come and get involved in the church someday when he got older. But then he added, "To tell you the truth, Jim, what I'm really hoping for is one of those neat deathbed conversions!" In his own way, he was saying, "God can be my co-pilot, but I really don't want to put him in the driver's seat—at least not yet, because I'm having too much fun."

Unfortunately, there are many people around today who think like that. They think of God as one who frowns on our fun, slaps our hands, and says, "Naughty, naughty! Mustn't do!" They think of Christianity as something old, negative, and prohibitive. For these people, religion does not give life; it takes life away. And they could not be more wrong!

What a gross misunderstanding of the Christian faith that is! We need always to remember that Christianity is *good* news! That's what the word *gospel* means—"good news," "glad tidings."

God is not only a comfort, he is a joy. He is the source of all pleasure. He is light and laughter. He is the Giver of Life—real life, abundant life, full life, meaningful life, joyful life, eternal life. And our chief purpose is to celebrate God, to serve him, and to enjoy him forever.

That's what the message in Matthew 6:33 is all about. Let me translate it like this: "Seek first the kingdom of God, and his righteousness and everything else will fall in place for you."

There is a scene from *Alice in Wonderland* where a lock with legs is running around in a panic. Frantically, the lock runs here, there, and everywhere. Finally, Alice says to the lock, "What are you doing? Why are you running around in all directions?" And the lock says, "I am seeking the key to unlock myself!"

And that is precisely what Jesus is giving us here in Matthew 6. He is saying, "Here it is! Here is the key that will unlock you. You don't have to run around in a panic all the time. Here is the key to life. Just celebrate God as the King of your life and the Lord of all your relationships. Let that be your number-one priority. Put that first, then everything else will fall into place for you, and your life will be full of joy and zest and purpose and mission and meaning and fulfillment."

Now, let me break this down a bit and bring it closer to home with three thoughts.

FIRST OF ALL, THE KEY TO LIFE IS TO SEEK GOD'S WILL

We can pray to God about anything. We can talk to God about our joys and our sorrows, our victories and our defeats, our blessings and our complaints, but the bottom-line prayer for the Christian is "Thy will, O God, be done."

Have you heard about the man who decided to write a book about the great churches of America? He decided to take a long trip across the country visiting the churches himself. He started in California. He was looking around and making photographs of a church in San Francisco when he noticed a golden telephone on a wall. Underneath the phone was a sign that read "$10,000 per minute." Intrigued, he found the pastor and asked about the golden phone. The pastor said, "Oh, that's a direct line to heaven, and if you want to use it, you can talk directly to God." "Thank you very much," the man said, and he continued on his way.

As he traveled across the country, he found the same golden phone with the same sign in Nevada, Arizona, Colorado, Illinois, Nebraska, and New York. At each site, he made the same inquiry about the golden phone and got the same answer.

Finally he arrived in Texas, and behold! He saw the same golden telephone with a sign. But this time the sign read "Free Calls." Fascinated, he found the pastor and said, "Pastor, I've been all across the nation and in many churches. I found a golden telephone like that on the wall there. And in each state, I was told it was a direct line to heaven, and that I could use it to speak directly to God for $10,000 a minute. But here, your sign reads 'Free Calls.' Why is that?" The pastor smiled and said, "Simple, my son. You are in Texas now, and it's a *local* call from here!"

Now, that story is a little "Texas humor." But the real truth is that it's a local call *anywhere*. Wherever we are, we have a direct line to heaven. Wherever we are, God is available and accessible. Wherever we are, it's a free local call! And we need to make lots of those calls seeking God's will for our lives.

We have a delightful member of our church who prays to God constantly. Her name is Katharin. She is 98 years young, and prayer is as natural to her as breathing. Like Tevye in *Fiddler on the Roof,* she just talks to God about everything. Once she said this to me: "Jim, when it comes to prayer, here's how I do it. I just say, 'Now Lord, here's what I want.' Then I tell him, 'I want this, I want that, and the other,' and then I say, 'But O Lord, have it *your* way, 'cause you're a lot smarter than I am.' " This was just Katharin's down-home way of saying "Thy will be done."

And she is so right! God is so much smarter than we are. God can see the big picture so much better than we can. So the key to life is, first of all, to seek God's will and follow it.

A SECOND KEY TO LIFE IS TO OBEY GOD'S WORD

As the old-timers used to say, "It's in the Book!" The key to life; the key to happiness; the key to morality; the key to ethics; the key to fulfillment can be found in the Bible, in the pages of Scripture. That's why the Bible is so important for us. It's our survival kit, our instruction manual, and our blueprint for building the kind of life God wants us to build. It has the answers that we long for and the solution we so desperately need to make life work. But our problem is that sometimes we are not sure we want God in the driver's seat. So we neglect the teachings of Scripture. We either fail to trust what the Bible teaches, or worse, we choose not to do what the Scriptures command.

Some years ago, a television program preceding the Winter Olympics featured some skiers who were blind learning to do slalom skiing. Each blind skier was paired up with a sighted skier. The blind skiers were taught on the flats how to make left and right turns by following the command of their sighted skiing partners. When this skill was mastered, they would go up to the slalom slope, where their sighted partners would ski beside them, shouting instructions at the appropriate moment: "Left!" "Right!" "Straight!" As they obeyed the commands, they were amazingly able to negotiate the difficult course and cross the finish line, depending solely on the sighted skiers' word. It was a situation of either complete trust or complete catastrophe.

That is a great parable for the Christian life. In this world we are often blind about what course to take, which way to turn. We must rely on the Word of the only One who is truly sighted, God himself. To avoid catastrophe, we follow his commands. His Word gives us the direction we need to finish the course. So if you are wondering about something—"Should I do this or not?"—look at the Ten Commandments (see Exodus 20:1-17)! If what you are contemplating violates any one of the Ten Commandments, then don't do it.

So, if you are trying to make a decision—"Should I do this or that or the other?"—look at Jesus, look at what he taught, look at what he stood for! If you cannot do what you are contemplating in the spirit of love, in the spirit of Jesus, then *don't do it!*

There is a wonderful true story about an American professor who traveled to London some years ago to do some post-doctorate study. While there, he attended the University Church of Christ the King in London. Sunday after Sunday as he worshiped, he was touched deeply by the beauty of the music—not only the singing of the choir, but also the singing of the congregation, especially from a cluster of people who sat near him in the back of the church.

One Sunday, he asked the minister who those people were. The minister told him that they were the cast of *Godspell,* which was playing in London at the time. He said that many of those young people had had no acquaintance with the Christian faith before they got into the cast of *Godspell.* But then, night after night, they sang the words from the Gospels, the words of *Godspell.* He said that the words had begun working on them. And so they had sought a place and a people who cared about those words, believed those words, followed those words, lived those words, and they had found that place and those people there at the church.

The point is clear: Once you get the words, once you understand what is being said in the gospel—the "Godspell"—then you want to be a part of it. You want to share it and live it and sing it. So, the key to life is to seek God's will and to obey God's Word.

THIRD AND FINALLY, THE KEY TO LIFE IS TO LIVE GOD'S WAY

Teacher and author Leo Buscaglia told a wonderful story about a student he had at Southern Cal some years ago. The student's name was Joel, and Joel was absolutely miserable. Joel felt useless and worthless and joyless. He was in depression. One day Joel told his professor, Leo Buscaglia, how unhappy and how unfulfilled he was. In despair, Joel said, "There is not one thing in my life that is worthwhile." Leo Buscaglia said, "Okay, Joel, let's go make a visit."

Buscaglia took Joel over to the convalescent hospital near the campus at Southern Cal. Inside, there were a lot of elderly people, lying on beds, staring at the ceiling. As they walked into that scene, Joel looked around and said, "What am I doing here? I don't know anything about gerontology."

Leo Buscaglia replied, "Good. You see that woman over there on the bed? Go over and say hello to her."

"That's all?" Joel asked.

"Yes, just go over there and say hello."

So Joel went over to the woman and said hello. She looked at him suspiciously. She asked, "Are you a relative?" Joel said, "No." And she said, "Good. Sit down."

So Joel sat down, and they started to talk. Buscaglia wrote:

Oh, the things she told him! This woman knew so much about love, pain, suffering. Even about approaching death, with which she had to make some kind of peace. But no one had cared about listening—until Joel.

Well, Joel started going to visit once a week. He was so regular that in the hospital they named that day "Joel's Day." Leo Buscaglia said that the greatest day in his teaching career was when he was walking across the campus one Saturday afternoon, and there was Joel, like a pied piper, with thirty older adults stretched out behind him. He was taking them to the coliseum to see a football game.

Somewhere in heaven, God was smiling, because that's God's way—that we find our life, our joy, our meaning, and our mission by reaching out in love to help other people.

Jesus put it like this: "Those who find their life will lose it, and those who lose their life for my sake will find it" (Matthew 10:39). In other words, the key to life is to seek God's will, to obey God's word, and to live God's way.

6

Celebrating God's Enduring Music

Making Music with What We Have Left

Scripture: Matthew 25:14-18

You may be familiar with the name Itzhak Perlman. He is one of the greatest violinists of all time. He was stricken with polio when he was a small child, but that has not stopped him. He has risen above that hurdle in his life with grace, grit, poise, and courage.

On November 18, 1995, Itzhak Perlman came on stage to give a concert at Lincoln Center in New York City. If you have ever been to a Perlman concert (or if you have ever seen one on television) you know that getting on stage is no small achievement for him. Because of the polio, he has heavy braces on both legs and walks with the aid of crutches. To see him walk across the stage one step at a time, painfully, slowly, arduously, is an awesome sight. He walks painfully, yet majestically, until he reaches his chair. Then he sits down, slowly puts his crutches on the floor, releases the clasps on his legs, tucks one foot back, and extends the other foot forward. Then he bends down, picks up his violin, puts it under his chin, nods to the director, and begins to play.

But this time, something went wrong. Just as he finished the first few bars, there was a loud *pop!* One of the strings on his violin broke! You could hear it snap all across the concert hall. Everybody in the room realized what had happened, and they all wondered, "What on earth is he going to do?" Most probably thought he would reattach his braces, pick up his crutches, and go looking for a new string or another violin. But he didn't. Perlman sat there for a moment, closed his eyes, and then amazingly, he signaled the conductor to begin again. The orchestra began, and Itzhak Perlman recomposed the piece in his head and played the entire piece with incredible power, passion, and purity on just three strings!

Now, we all would think that's impossible. We know that can't be done. I know that, and you know that, but that night, Itzhak Perlman refused to know that. You could see him modulating, changing, rethinking the piece in his head and playing it perfectly on the three strings he had left. When he finished, there was an awesome silence in the room. And then people rose and cheered wildly, an extraordinary outburst of applause from every corner of the auditorium. People were on their feet, screaming, cheering, clapping, doing everything they could to show how much they appreciated what he had just done.

Itzhak Perlman smiled, wiped the sweat from his brow, raised his violin bow to quiet the crowd, and then—not boastfully but in a quiet, pensive, reverent tone—he said (and I paraphrase): "Sometimes it is the artist's task to find out how much music you can still make with what you have left."

Isn't that a great line and a powerful thought? Commenting about that, Jack Reimer wrote: "Perhaps that is the way of life—not just for artists but for all of us. Here is a man who has prepared all his life to make music on a violin of four strings, who, all of a sudden, in the middle of a concert, finds himself with only three strings. So he makes music with three strings, and the music he made that night with just three strings was more beautiful, more sacred, more memorable, than any he had ever made before, when he had four strings. So, perhaps our task in this shaky, fast-changing, bewildering world in which we live is to make music, at first with all that we have and then, when that is no longer possible, to make music with what we have left" (*Chicken Soup for the Soul, Houston Chronicle* 2/17/01).

What a great lesson for us to learn, because the truth is that so many people in life today are like that one-talent servant in Matthew 25. They don't like what they have left, so in bitterness, in apathy, in disillusionment, they throw up their hands in dismay, throw in the towel in defeat, and quit on life, crying, "Life is not fair to me!" "Life has given me a raw deal!" "Life has favored others more than me, so I'll show 'em. I just won't play!" So they bury their talent in the ground, and the music in their life stops. That is so sad, and so unnecessary.

I don't know about you, but I get a kick out of country music. The titles of the songs and the lyrics are sometimes pretty earthy and often have a self-deprecating humor. For example, there is the classic "I've Got Tears in My Ears from Lying on My Back and Crying My Eyes Out Over You."

Then there's that "romantic" ballad "You Done Tore My Heart Out and Stomped That Sucker Flat." There is the tender love song "King Kong Was Just a Little Ol' Monkey Compared to My Love for You." I love this one: "If You Leave Me, Walk Out Backwards, So I'll Think You're Coming In."

But every now and then, a country song will come along that has a great melody and a powerful message. A good example of that is the award-winning hit "I Hope You Dance," which was sung by Lee Ann Womack. It was the Country Music Song of the Year, and in 2001 it won a Grammy for Best Country Song. I had heard it a number of times but hadn't really listened to the words until one morning. It was then that I realized that this song has the same message that we find in the parable of the talents in Matthew 25: Don't quit on life. Don't get bitter. Don't get disillusioned. Keep on making music with what you have left. Keep on dancing. Keep on celebrating life.

This is the calling of every Christian, isn't it? To do our best and trust God for the rest. To keep on singing, to keep on dancing, to keep on celebrating life, come what may. To make music at first with all that we have, and then, when circumstances change, to make music with what we have left.

Let me bring this closer to home with three thoughts.

FIRST OF ALL, AFTER A BIG DISAPPOINTMENT, WE ARE CALLED TO MAKE MUSIC WITH WHAT WE HAVE LEFT

Disappointment is a fact of living. As J. Wallace Hamilton once put it, "Every person's life is a diary in which he or she means to write one story and is forced to write yet another."

Milton went blind.

Beethoven lost his hearing.

Pasteur became a paralytic at 46.

Helen Keller was deaf, blind, and unable to speak intelligibly.

The apostle Paul wanted to go to Spain to start the

Christian church there but instead was thrown into prison in Rome.

But were these persons defeated by these disappointments? Absolutely not! They all, each and every one of them, turned their disappointments into the instruments of victory. With the help of God, we can do that too. Indeed, this is the calling of every Christian—to turn defeats into victories! If you ever wonder about that, just remember that the central symbol of our faith is a cross. Leslie Weatherhead put it powerfully like this: "The cross looked like defeat to the disciples, it was called defeat by the world, it must have felt like defeat to Jesus, but God made it his greatest victory."

Some years ago, a young man dreamed of becoming a Christian missionary. He wanted to share the gospel of Christ with the world. He was accepted and assigned to go to a remote mission post in Africa. But when he reported to the mission board in New York to arrange for his passage to Africa, he was required to take one more physical exam, and he flunked it. It was discovered that he and his wife would not be able to withstand the climate in Africa where the mission station was located.

He was so disappointed, so crestfallen. He began to pray to God, asking that God would give him a new plan and a new direction for his life. He returned home to Ohio. He joined his father, a reformed alcoholic, in experimenting with a non-alcoholic wine that could be used for communion in their local church.

This little experimental juice was just what the church needed. With the support of his pastor, the young man went into business to sell and market his brand-new product. He called it Welch's Grape Juice. Proceeds from the sale of the communion juice went to the Methodist Mission Field. In his major disappointment, he found his Christian mission, because even after that big disappointment, he kept on making music with what he had left.

SECOND, AFTER A PAINFUL HEARTACHE, WE ARE CALLED TO MAKE MUSIC WITH WHAT WE HAVE LEFT

Madelyn Hildreth is a friend of mine. She is without question one of the outstanding book reviewers in our nation. She is also an inspiration to everyone who knows her, not just because of her brilliant talent as a reviewer of books, but even more because of her inner strength, her determination, and her great Christian attitudes, which have enabled her to overcome polio. Like Itzhak Perlman, she too was stricken with polio as a child. Listen to her words: "When I was three years old, I was one of the first nine people to have the disease diagnosed as polio in New York state, and I was nearly sixteen before a series of long hospital stays and endless operations enabled me to put my feet on the floor, and with the aid of heavy braces and crutches, to begin to walk. I've never been able to walk across an open field or play a game of tennis, or go to a dance.

"I know the meaning of frustration. I've had to work hard on my attitudes. I could not permit myself to be eaten up by the virus of self-pity—or jealousy for those who possessed something without any effort that I have worked my head off to gain—and know now I will never have. I have lived in a prison cell, in a body that I could not control. What am I to do? How am I to respond? The Christian answer is to move forward! If life gives us a lemon, then with the help of God we must make it into a refreshing lemonade."

And that is exactly what Madelyn Hildreth has done. After a painful heartache, she refused to quit. She refused to give up. She refused to bury her talent in the ground. She has kept on making music with what she had left.

THIRD AND FINALLY, AFTER A GREAT SORROW, WE ARE CALLED TO MAKE MUSIC WITH WHAT WE HAVE LEFT

Some time ago, we had a memorial service in our sanctuary for one of the finest men I have ever known. He could light up a room just by walking in. He could make you smile and feel good about life with his unflappable sense of humor, his warm touch, and his radiant smile. He could make you feel like he had been waiting all day just for this moment to get to be with you. His name was Bill Landes. Well, actually, his name was Morris Homer Landes, but when he was sixteen years old, he realized that life could be tough for a teenager named Morris Homer, so one day he just changed his name to Bill.

A little over ten years ago, Bill was hit with a devastating eye problem, and pretty quickly he lost his vision in one eye and then the other. And so for the last ten years of his life, he was legally blind. That was a great sorrow for him, because it meant that he could never again do so many of the things he loved to do. He couldn't play golf anymore. He couldn't drive a car anymore. He couldn't get out and do the community service he enjoyed so much.

It was a perfect formula for depression, bitterness, and disillusionment. But not so for Bill Landes! He kept on making music with what he had left. He kept on making music with his faith, his hope, his love, and his remarkable, off-the-wall sense of humor. He once told me that his favorite salad was the Honeymoon Salad. I bit, and asked, "What's a Honeymoon Salad?" He said, "Lettuce alone!"

Bill Landes was a remarkable man who knew disappointment and heartache and sorrow, but he refused to be bowled over. He refused to give up. He refused to quit. He refused to wallow in self-pity. He refused to complain. No, instead he kept on making his special brand of music, he kept on dancing, he kept on celebrating life and love.

That's our calling as Christians, isn't it—no matter how many disappointments and heartaches and sorrows come our way, to keep on making music with what we have left.

7

Celebrating God's Greatest Promise

"Remember, I Am with You Always"

Scripture: Matthew 28:16-20

We have all heard the haunting melody of "Taps." The poignant sound of "Taps" being played by a lone bugler somewhere off in the distance can put a lump in our throats and bring tears to our eyes. There is a beautiful legend about the origin of this song. Have you heard it?

It is set in 1862 during the Civil War. Union Army Captain Robert Ellicombe was on the front lines with his men near Harrison's Landing in Virginia. The Confederate Army was on the other side of the narrow strip of land. During the night, Captain Ellicombe heard a painful sound, the moans of a soldier who was severely wounded on the battlefield. He did not know if the injured man was one of his, a Union soldier, or one of the enemy, a Confederate soldier. But still those cries for help were so heartwrenching that Captain Ellicombe decided to risk his own life and go out and bring the injured man back for medical attention.

Crawling on his stomach through the gunfire, the captain reached the wounded soldier and pulled him back toward the Union soldier's encampment. When they finally made it back to camp, Captain Ellicombe discovered that the young man was actually a Confederate soldier, and that the soldier was by now dead.

The captain lit a lantern and suddenly gasped for breath, numb with shock. In the dim light of the lantern, he saw the face of the soldier, a face he knew so very well. It was his own son! The young man had been studying music in the South when the war broke out. Without telling his father, the boy had enlisted in the Confederate Army and now had been killed at the Battle of Harrison's Landing. Captain Ellicombe was absolutely heartbroken. The next morning, the captain asked his superiors for permission to give his son a full military burial with an Army band there to play the service, despite the fact that his son was in the Confederate Army.

His request was denied. But out of respect for the dead soldier's father, permission was granted to give him one musician. The captain chose a bugler. And he asked the bugler to play a series of musical notes that he had found on a piece of paper in the pocket of his son's uniform. The wish was granted, and the bugler played the notes just as they were written; and the haunting melody of "Taps" was born.

Now, though the song has a sad and sorrowful sound, it also has verses (there are several popular versions, though none is "official") that resound with the good news of the Bible. The words remind us that God is always with us, that nothing, not even death, can separate us from God and His love:

> Day is done, gone the sun,
> From the hills, from the lake, from the skies.
> All is well, safely rest,
> God is nigh.

Most of us probably have felt chills running up and down our spine while listening to the sound of "Taps," but really, the thrill here is found in the words. Read again the last lines: *All is well, safely rest, God is nigh.*

God is always near. God is always here. God is always in charge. God is always with us, wherever we may be. That's the thrilling thing about this song. It's the same message the risen Christ was giving in Matthew 28, when he said, "Remember, I am with you always, to the end of the age" (verse 20). When you study the Bible closely, you discover this promise of God to always be with us repeated over and over again, on page after page of our Scriptures. When you study the Gospels closely, you discover that there are numerous accounts of Resurrection appearances—all exciting, all amazing, all mind-boggling.

For example, the risen Christ appeared to Mary in the garden on Easter morning, giving her the good news she needed.

He appeared dramatically to the disciples in the Upper Room, giving them the encouragement they needed.

He appeared again to Doubting Thomas, giving him the assurance he needed.

He appeared to those two disillusioned men on the Emmaus road, giving them the hope they needed.

He appeared to Simon Peter on the seashore, giving him the forgiveness he so desperately needed.

And here in Matthew 28, we see yet another Resurrection appearance. Christ appeared to the disciples on a mountaintop in Galilee, giving them—and us—the Great Promise we need, the promise to always be with us. "Remember, I am with you always."

A few years ago, a schoolteacher asked her pupils, "Who is the greatest living person?" Some wrote the name of President Carter, some President Bush, some General Schwarzkopf, some Mother Teresa, and some Billy Graham. And some wrote the names of other prominent people of the time. One boy even wrote "Joe Montana." But one little girl wrote "Jesus." Noting this last answer, the teacher replied, "I said *'living* person.'" "But, he *is* living!" the little girl insisted. Many of us would agree with this perceptive little girl—Jesus Christ is alive today!

However, many "believers" are not sure where Christ can be found. Once, two little girls were studying a portrait of Queen Victoria sitting on her throne. "What's she doing?" one of them asked. The other gazed hard at the picture, and then she said, "Oh, nothing. She's just sitting there reigning."

Let me ask you something: Is that your view of Jesus Christ—a distant king, just sitting upon a celestial throne, far removed from the problems of the world, just sitting there, reigning? This is not the portrait the Bible presents of the Living Savior. This is not the good news of the Christian faith. Christ said, "Remember, I am with you always." What does that mean? Where can his presence be felt? Well, in a sense, he is everywhere, but his personal presence is especially felt, and his personal power especially evident, in the following three places.

FIRST OF ALL, WE CAN FIND HIM WHEREVER HIS PEOPLE ARE WORSHIPING

Remember how the Bible puts it. In Matthew 18, Jesus says, "For where two or three are gathered in my name, I am there among them" (verse 20).

The phone rang in the office of a Washington church one Sunday morning. The voice asked, "Will the President be in church today?" The pastor quickly replied, "That I cannot promise, but I do know this: Jesus Christ will be here, and that should be sufficient incentive for a reasonably large attendance."

When the Queen of England toured Canada some years ago, she attended a little church in Niagara Falls. Before the service began, people jammed the auditorium and filled the church lawn with the hope of getting a glimpse of the queen. But consider this: Jesus Christ, the King of kings has promised to attend every service where two or three gather in his name, and yet we take that promise so lightly, don't we? We make it to church if and when it's convenient. We make it to church if and when we can work it into our busy schedule.

I'm sure there are many places to get a glimpse of the risen Christ, but the best place is in your church. Wherever people are worshiping, the risen Christ is there!

SECOND, WE CAN FIND HIM WHEREVER HIS PEOPLE ARE SERVING

In Matthew 28, the risen Christ gives us a job. He puts us to work. He tells us to go out into the world—preaching, teaching, baptizing—and then he adds that great promise: "Remember, I am with you always."

After sixteen very difficult years of service as a missionary in the heart of Africa, David Livingstone returned to his native land of Scotland. During his furlough, he was asked to speak to the students at Glasgow

University. His body was weakened and emaciated from his experience. If you think the TV *Survivors* have it rough for the 42 or so days they are on their adventure, let me tell you what happened to David Livingstone.

Over sixteen years in Africa, he suffered and survived twenty-seven bouts with tropical fever. One of his arms hung motionless at his side, the result of being mangled by a lion. As he stood before those students at the university, he said, "I will tell you what sustained me amidst the toil, the hardship, the suffering, and the loneliness. It was Christ's promise, 'Lo, I am with you always' " (RSV).

One of the most convincing proofs of a living Christ is the unselfish service of his people. And Christians will tell you that they never feel a greater consciousness of the Lord's presence than when they are serving him by sharing their faith and love with others.

Wherever people are worshiping, wherever people are serving, the risen Lord is there.

THERE IS A THIRD PLACE WHERE WE CAN FIND CHRIST: WHEREVER HIS PEOPLE ARE SUFFERING, THE RISEN LORD IS THERE

At first glance, it seems like it would be so easy to find Christ in the beautiful, sacred, lovely places of life, or in those situations where all the breaks are going our way. But the truth is that the risen Lord is never nearer to us than when we are hurting. Time after time, I have heard people say it, "This is the hardest thing we've ever gone through; our hearts are broken, but we will be all right because God is with us as never before."

Notice those last three words? *As never before*—"God is with us *as never before*." Why do we feel his presence with us so vividly when we are suffering? Probably for two reasons.

First, when we are hurting, we are more open to him. We are more willing and anxious and ready for him to come and help us. And second, God is like a loving parent, and all good, loving parents want to be with their children when they are hurting. When our children are suffering, everything else goes on the back burner.

Once I was at the hospital visiting a little girl who was very sick. Her mother had been at her bedside for days and days. The doctor called me out into the hallway and said, "Jim, see if you can get that young mother to go home for a while. She hasn't slept, she hasn't eaten, and she's got to be exhausted. See if you can get her to go home." I went back in and said, "Why don't you come and let me take you home for a while?" She looked up at me and said, "Jim, you don't really want me to leave her when she is this sick, do you?" Being a parent myself, I understood. "No," I said. "Let me go downstairs and get you a sandwich."

God is like that—a loving parent who wants to be especially close to his children when they are suffering. Isn't it something, how we can find the risen Lord wherever his people are worshiping, wherever his people are serving, and wherever his people are suffering.

8
Celebrating God's Healing Love
Heartprints

Scripture: John 15:12-14

Some years ago, the noted writer Norman Cousins wrote a book called *The Healing Heart*. It was written out of his own personal experience of having and surviving a heart attack. In the book, he gives great accolades to the highly proficient and multitalented doctors of our time. But he also states that while some doctors today are brilliant technicians, brilliant scientists, they are not all "people persons." Many, he says, have no training at all in the art of communication, no training at all in relating warmly to their patients, and consequently, he says, "they don't realize how the hospital patients look so forward to their visits and hang on their every word."

Now, I'm sure that Norman Cousins had a point that medical schools should take seriously, but I must hurry to tell you that I have not found that to be true with the doctors I know in my city and church. With so many of them, you get the best of both worlds! You get a doctor with a bright mind and talented hands, but also a warm and compassionate heart. You get a physician and a pastor all rolled into one!

A case in point was documented for me last week. One of our finest doctors had a moving and touching experience with one of his patients. The doctor is a highly respected heart surgeon, and he had helped this patient with her medical problem. And knowing this doctor as I do, I'm sure that he also had befriended her with his warm and compassionate Christian spirit. To express her gratitude, the patient gave her doctor a gift. The gift was a beautiful ceramic heart (a fitting gift for a heart doctor), and attached to the gift was a beautiful message, a prayer poem entitled "Heartprints." Listen to these words:

> Whatever our hands touch—
> We leave fingerprints!
> On walls, on furniture,
> On doorknobs, dishes, books,
> As we touch we leave our identity.
>
> O God, wherever I go today,
> Help me to leave heartprints!
> Heartprints of compassion,
> Of understanding and love.
> Heartprints of kindness
> And genuine concern.
>
> May my heart touch a lonely neighbor,
> Or a runaway daughter,
> Or an anxious mother,
> Or, perhaps, a dear friend!
>
> Lord, send me out today
> To leave heartprints.
> And if anyone should say,
> "I felt your touch,"
> May that one sense thy love
> Touching through me.

Now, that prayer poem, "Heartprints," simply underscores something the Bible has been telling us all along;

namely, that there is nothing in the world more powerful than the healing power of love. Sometimes we forget that or wonder about it, maybe even doubt it. We want to put our faith in military power and intellectual pursuits and scientific advances and economic strength and international alliances and political clout.

But over and over, the Scriptures tell us that love is the answer, that love is the will of God for us, that love is the single most authentic sign of discipleship, that love is the hope of the world. Here in John 15, we see it again. Jesus said, "This is my commandment, that you love one another as I have loved you. No one has greater love than this, to lay down one's life for one's friends" (verses 12-13).

Jesus was the Great Physician, and he knew full well the healing power of love. Let's look at that now, the incredible, amazing, awesome, healing power of love. Dr. Karl Menninger, the well-known psychiatrist, once said that he believes the most tragic word in human language today is the word *unloved*. Feeling unloved— there's nothing worse than that, nothing more devastating than that, nothing more destructive than that. Dr. Menninger went on to say that on the other hand, "Love has the power to cure people—both the ones who give it and the ones who receive it." And he's right. Love *can* cure. The heartprints of love can restore and mend and heal.

Now, let me be more specific.

FIRST OF ALL, LOVE HAS THE POWER TO HEAL US PHYSICALLY

Scientific research is now confirming what many of us have suspected all along—that love plays a big part in the healing of a hurting body.

Some years ago, Roy Angell told the story about a particularly affectionate puppy that liked to hang out around a sanitarium. A doctor at the sanitarium decided to try an experiment on the pup. She made a small incision on the puppy's leg. Then she bandaged it. Finally, she instructed those at the sanitarium to feed the puppy when he was hungry, but not to show him any affection physically or verbally. The change in the little dog was quick and dramatic. Whereas before he had always been energetic, frisky, happy, and friendly, he now seemed quite forlorn and pitiful. Even more significant, six weeks later the incision on his leg had not healed.

The doctor then instructed everyone at the sanitarium to do just the opposite—to lavish love on the little puppy, to speak kindly to him, to hold him, pet him, stroke him, and love him. Amazingly, soon the puppy was frisky and happy and energetic again. And the incision healed very quickly. The point is clear: The healing streams that lie within the body, which may be energized and activated by the power of love, are potent indeed, more so perhaps than we even realize.

A few years ago in Sweden, a nurse working in a government hospital was assigned to an elderly woman patient. This patient was a tough case. She had not spoken a word in three years. The other nurses disliked her and tried to avoid her as much as they could. Basically, they ignored her. But the new nurse decided to try "unconditional love." The patient rocked all day in a rocking chair. So one day, the nurse pulled up a rocking chair beside the patient and just rocked along with her, and loved her. Occasionally, the nurse would reach over and gently touch and pat the hand of the woman.

After just a few days of this, the patient suddenly

opened her eyes, turned, and said to the nurse, "You're so kind." The next day, she talked more, and incredibly, two weeks later, the patient was well enough to leave the hospital and go home! Of course, it doesn't always work like that, but studies are accumulating that show, without question, that love has healing power.

Take for example the poet Elizabeth Barrett. She was an invalid for many years, unable even to lift her head from her pillow. But then, one day she was visited by a man named Robert Browning. It was love at first sight. In just one visit, he brought her so much joy and happiness that she lifted her head. On his second visit, she sat up in bed. On the third visit, they eloped!

Love can heal us physically! No wonder people were healed by coming into physical contact with Jesus. He was love incarnate. And that's what he is calling us to be—today's love made flesh. Love personified. Love lived out.

This is the first point. Love can heal bodies. Love can heal us physically.

SECOND, LOVE HAS THE POWER TO HEAL US EMOTIONALLY

Some years ago, when I was serving a church in another state, a man and his wife came to see me one day. They were burdened, worried, troubled. It was obvious. I could tell that they both had been crying. The man spoke first: "It's our daughter, Betty. She's eighteen years old now, and we are worried sick about her. She has absolutely no self-esteem at all, and she has gotten a reputation around town."

"Reputation?" I asked. "What do you mean?"

"Well," said the man painfully, "her self-esteem is so low that any time any man pays attention to her" (his voice trailed off, and he began to sob). Then the doctor's wife said it bluntly: "Jim, she can't say no to any man, and now, she has this horrible reputation. It's all over town. We're worried sick, and we're scared. We're at the end of our rope. We don't know what to do with her. She's emotionally ill. She needs help."

Well, I met with Betty, and they were right about her self-esteem. It was nonexistent. She walked all slumped over. Her hair was dirty and scraggly, her clothes unkempt and out of style. She wore no makeup. She could not look me in the eye. Most of the time she stared at the floor, and when she looked up, her eyes darted like a scared rabbit. She was in a pitiful state. She looked like that Ruth Buzzi character on the old *Laugh-In* TV show. I brought in a psychiatrist. We both worked with her, but to be honest we didn't make much progress at all. It seemed hopeless.

But then, the most amazing thing happened. A new young man named Jerry moved to town. He was the son of a pastor, and he fell in love with Betty. He said, "Betty, I know about your past. I know about your reputation. I know the names they call you. I've heard all the rumors, but I also know that I love you, and you are so beautiful to me!" He kept telling her, "I love you, and you are so beautiful." And pretty soon, she started believing him. She began to stand up straight. She put on a little makeup. She combed her hair. She bought some new clothes. And she did something else I'd never seen her do before: She started smiling!

Not long after, I performed their wedding, and then shortly thereafter I moved away to another city. A couple of years later, I was invited to come back to that church to preach one Sunday morning. As I walked toward the sanctuary, I passed through the children's building, and I saw Jerry coming out of a Sunday-school classroom. He had been teaching the fourth grade. With him was a gorgeous woman. She looked like a model—tall, stately, poised, radiant—and I thought: *O my goodness, Jerry has left Betty and found somebody else.* But I was wrong!

As I drew closer to them, I realized that the gorgeous, radiant, confident woman who had been helping Jerry teach the children in Sunday school was none other than Betty herself! I could hardly believe my eyes, and deep down in my heart I hummed the Doxology! Betty had been transformed. She had been restored. She had been made well. She had been healed by love!

Love has the power to heal us, both physically and emotionally.

THIRD AND FINALLY, LOVE HAS THE POWER TO HEAL US SPIRITUALLY

A well-known speaker started off his seminar by holding up a crisp, new $20 bill. There were 200 people in the room. The speaker asked them, "How many of you would like to have this $20 bill?" Hands went up all over the room. Then the speaker said, "I'm going to give this $20 bill to one of you, but first let me do this." He proceeded to crumple the $20 bill, and then he held it up and said, "Who wants it now?" Hands went up everywhere. "Well," he replied, "What if I do this?" He dropped it on the ground and stepped on it, and started to grind it into the floor with his shoe. He picked it up and held it up for all to see. It was crumpled and smudged and dirty, and he said, "Who wants it now?" Still, hands went up all over the place. Then the speaker said, "My friends, you have just learned a very valuable lesson. No matter what I did to the money, you still wanted it because it did not decrease in value. No matter how smudged and rumpled it became, it was still worth $20."

Many times in our lives, we get knocked around—dropped, crumpled, smudged, and ground into the dirt—by the decisions we make and the circumstances that come our way. And sometimes we feel as though we are worthless and used up and of no account. But no matter what has happened or what will happen, you will never lose your value in God's eyes. To God, dirty or clean, crumpled or finely creased, you are still priceless! The psalmist in Psalm 17:8 asks God to guard him as the apple of God's eye. And God will always keep *us* as the apple of his eye, not because we are good, but because *God* is good. That is God's amazing grace, and that is the only way spiritual healing can happen.

In his book *Come Share the Being,* Bob Benson writes about God's incredible grace and the amazing ways in which God shares himself with us. He writes:

Do you remember when they had old fashioned Sunday school picnics? It was before air-conditioning. They said, "We'll meet at Sycamore Lodge in Shelby Park at 4:30 Saturday. You bring your supper and we'll furnish the tea."

But you came home at the last minute and when you got ready to pack your lunch, all you could find in the refrigerator was one dried up piece of baloney and just enough mustard in the bottom of the jar so that you got it all over your knuckles trying to get to it. And there were just two stale pieces of bread. So you made your baloney sandwich and wrapped it in some brown bag and went to the picnic. And when it came time to eat you sat at the end of a table and spread out your sandwich.

But the folks next to you—the lady was a good cook and she had worked all day and she had fried chicken, and baked beans, and potato salad, and homemade rolls, and sliced tomatoes, and pickles, and olives, and celery, and topped it off with two big homemade chocolate pies. And they spread it all out beside you and there you were with your baloney sandwich. But they said to you, "Why don't we put it all together?" "No, I couldn't do that, I just couldn't even think of it," you murmured embarrassedly. "Oh, come on, there's plenty of chicken and plenty of pie, and plenty of everything—and we just love baloney sandwiches. Let's put it all together." And so you did and there you sat—eating like a king when you came like a pauper.

The point is obvious: We bring our little, and God brings his much, and in his amazing grace, God says "Let's put it all together." If we will only accept it in faith, God has a banquet for us when we are hungry. God has healing for us when we are hurting. God can satisfy the hollow emptiness within us. God can make the wounded whole. God can heal the sin-sick soul, through the power, the healing power, of his love!

9

Celebrating God's Call to Discipleship

Wanted: Great Followers

Scripture: Mark 1:16-20

Have you heard about the animals in the jungle who got together one day and decided to play a football game? They chose sides, and one team learned pretty quickly that they had (if you will pardon the pun) a *big* problem. The rhinoceros was on the other team, and they simply could not tackle him. They tried, but they just bounced off. Every time the rhinoceros got the ball he ran right down the middle of the field, and they couldn't stop him. In the first quarter the rhinoceros scored a touchdown. Then, in the second quarter he scored again, and then again in the third quarter. They tried to keep the ball away from him, but every time the rhinoceros touched the ball, he ran for a touchdown.

Finally, with just a few minutes left in the game, the rhinoceros caught the ball one more time and started up the field. Suddenly, out of nowhere, he was brought down with a magnificent tackle. When the animals unpiled, it was discovered that the centipede had (for the first time) finally come into the game, and that it was, indeed, the centipede who had made the tackle. "That was fantastic!" shouted his teammates. "Great tackle! But look, it's the fourth quarter, and the game is almost over!

Where on earth have you been all this time?" The centipede answered, "I was putting on my shoes!"

Many people are like that—and worse! They go through life just "putting on their shoes," "getting ready to do something" but never making a start; preparing, wanting to do something, but somehow never getting around to doing it.

In Mark 1, as Jesus says "Follow me," he is calling us to action! To Simon (Peter), Andrew, James, and John he was saying—and to each one of us he is saying, "Put on your shoes! Take the field! Join the struggle! Get off the sidelines, and get into the game! Follow me! I've got a job for you! Follow me, and count for something!"

Now, the word *follow* is a powerful word in the Scriptures. The Greek word for *follow* in the New Testament is *akoloutheo*, and it carries a strong meaning. It means obedience, the kind of obedience a soldier gives his commanding officer. It means commitment, the kind of commitment that is unflinching, unwavering, and unshakable. It means love, the kind of love that is total, sacrificial, and complete. It means devotion, devotion to a great cause, a cause outside yourself and larger than yourself.

This is serious business here! Jesus is giving the call to discipleship. When Jesus says "Follow me," he doesn't mean "Let's walk around the corner together," or "Let's jog back to town together." He is playing for keeps! He is asking for our devotion, our trust, our service, our loyalty. He is asking for our lives, our hearts, our souls, our minds, and our strength. He is calling us to be his disciples. "Follow me!" he says. "Follow me"; ancient, stirring, time-honored, universal, provocative, challenging words. Words to mull over and meditate upon and hear afresh. Words to motivate and challenge and inspire. Words to respond to with faith and hope and obedience.

Actually, Jesus said these words not once, but many times: to Peter and Andrew, there by the sea; to Matthew at the tax-collection table (Matthew 9:9); to a hesitant, would-be disciple on the roadside (Matthew 8:21-22); to the rich young ruler (Luke 18:18-30); and now, this moment, to you and me. Can you hear him? If you will listen closely, he is speaking loud and clear, and he is saying, "Deny yourself! Take up your cross! Follow me! Put on your shoes and get in the game!"

There are some considerations that have moved me in recent days to a new appreciation of these words. Let me list a few of them and invite you to think with me about these three thoughts. When Jesus says "Follow me," he is calling us to a new direction, a new future, and a new lifestyle. Now, let's take a look at these one at a time.

FIRST, WHEN JESUS SAYS, "FOLLOW ME," HE IS CALLING US TO A NEW DIRECTION

A new direction. Anyone who says "follow me" is going somewhere, and he wants us to go with him. This is really good news for us, because oh, how we need a sense of direction!

On a recent vacation, I was walking on the beach one morning when I saw a teenager wearing a T-shirt, which had these words on the back: *Don't Follow Me, I'm Lost!* Now, of course that young man was wearing that T-shirt as a joke, and when I read those words on his back, I smiled. But listen—being lost is really no joke! Have you ever been lost? It's a horrible feeling, a panicky, frightening, empty feeling. You don't know which way to go, which way to turn. You have no sense of direction, and you feel so helpless and so hopeless. Many people live in a constant state of "lost-ness."

Not long ago, I visited with a young man in his late twenties who said, "I am so mixed up and frustrated. I feel I'm at loose ends, with absolutely no sense of direction or purpose. Another year has passed, and I feel that I'm just spinning my wheels. My life is going nowhere." Let me ask you something. Do you ever feel like that? Like you're just spinning your wheels and your life is going nowhere? I wonder if Simon, Andrew, James, and John were feeling that way before Jesus walked into their lives that day.

Every one of us needs a reason to get up in the morning. So, let me ask you: What's yours? What is it that makes you spring out of bed in the morning with energy and excitement? As human beings, we hunger for meaning and purpose and direction in our lives. At the very core of who we are, we need to feel that our lives do make a difference. We all need a reason, a good reason, to get up in the morning. We need to feel a sense of purpose. Listen! If you feel empty inside, if you feel lost or bored or mixed up, let me invite you with all the feeling in my heart to follow Jesus Christ. He is the way, the truth, and the life!

There's an old story about the man who hired a native guide to lead him through the jungles of Africa. As the wilderness became more and more dense, the man got nervous, and he said to the guide, "Are you sure you know where we are going? You have no map, no compass, and there is no path!" The guide answered, "My friend, in this jungle, I am the path! Just stay close and follow me." When Jesus calls us to follow him, that's what he is saying to us: "In this jungle wilderness of a world, I am the way, the truth, the life, and the path. I'll show you a new direction. Follow me, and I will see you through."

SECOND, WHEN JESUS SAYS, "FOLLOW ME," HE IS CALLING US TO A NEW FUTURE

Anyone who says "follow me" is obviously more interested in the future than in the past. Jesus certainly is. With Jesus, it's not where you've been, but where you're going; not whether you have fallen, but whether you will get up; not whom you have hurt in the past, but whom you will help in the future.

In recent years, a new approach to psychiatry has emerged called "reality therapy." Its founding mentor was William Glasser. The approach is a little blunt, but it makes sense to me. Reality therapists will not let us spend a lot of time rummaging around in the past. Rather, they say, "So you have a problem? So you've failed? So you've been hurt? So what? Everybody has problems! Now, what are you going to do about it?"

It is interesting to note in the Bible how little time Jesus spent talking with people about their past. He was more interested in their future. When the woman who had been caught in adultery was brought to him, Jesus did not explore the circumstances that had pushed her to her fall. He simply took her by the hand and said, "Neither do I condemn you. Go your way, and from now on do not sin again" (John 8:11).

When Nicodemus came to him under the cover of night, shackled by an impossible legalism, Jesus didn't ask him how he got that way or fuss at him for being that way, but rather he simply answered Nicodemus' question, telling him that the way to heaven was to be "born again," or "born from above" (see John 3:3).

And nowhere is Jesus' emphasis on the importance of the future over the past more beautifully depicted than in his parable of the prodigal son (Luke 15:11-32). The father doesn't even let the lost son finish his confession, doesn't want to hear it. He wants to get on with the party.

This too is the good news of our faith. We don't have to be defeated by the hurts or failings or sins of the past. We can be forgiven. We can start over. We can make a new beginning. The Savior comes forgiving us and calling us to a new direction and a new future.

THIRD, WHEN JESUS SAYS, "FOLLOW ME," HE IS CALLING US TO A NEW LIFESTYLE

Jesus is calling us away from selfishness and to the spirit of Christlike love. That is the lifestyle of the Christian disciple—to live every day in the spirit of self-giving, sacrificial love.

Dr. E. V. Hill is a beloved pastor serving a church in the Watts area of Los Angeles. During the burnings, lootings, and community riots there in the 1960s, Dr. Hill had to do a very painful thing. He had to stand tall and speak out against his neighbors who were destroying property and stealing from area merchants. During the worst part of the rioting, that kind of preaching brought threats to him and his church. It was a tough time. Tension crackled in the air, and the threats against Dr. Hill became more numerous and more severe.

One night his telephone rang, and his wife noticed how serious and solemn he was after that call. "What was that all about?" she asked.

"Oh nothing," he answered.

She pressed him, "You have to tell me."

"I don't want you to worry," he said.

"It was a threat, wasn't it?"

Finally, he told her. "They have threatened to blow up our car with me in it." The couple held one another tightly. They cried. They prayed. They realized that they couldn't possibly guard the car and protect it from wire bombings twenty-four hours a day.

The next morning, Dr. Hill went into the kitchen and noticed that his wife was not in the house, and neither was his automobile in the carport. He became alarmed, but a few minutes later his wife came walking in the back door. "Where have you been?" he asked her.

She said, "I drove the car around the block to make sure it would be safe for you to drive it to work this morning!" Dr. Hill said that from that day on, he never, ever, had to ask his wife again if she loved him. He saw her love in action.

And that's what the world needs from us! They will know we are Christians, they will know that we are followers of Jesus Christ, by our love. More than ever before, the world needs to see us follow Jesus Christ to a new direction, to a new future, and to a new lifestyle of unselfish love.

10

Celebrating God's Three Ways of Acting

Every Belief Was First a Song

Scripture: Psalm 95:1-7

Recently, I read about some high school sophomores who were asked by their English teacher to write a definition of *love*. The teacher said that some of the answers were not so much definitions as they were "daffynitions." For example, one student wrote, "Love is the feeling in your stomach of butterflies wearing roller skates." Another said, "Life is one thing after another! Love is two things after each other!" But here is my favorite. A student wrote these profound words: "Love is that feeling you feel when you feel you are going to have a feeling like you have never felt before!" Now, that's a definition, isn't it?

The point is that love is terribly difficult to define. Something that powerful and wonderful defies description. Words aren't big enough. It is so deep, so amazing, so awesome that it is just hard to put it into words. It's hard to define love, but we have all experienced it, haven't we? The same thing is true with some of our basic Christian beliefs. Take, for example, the doctrine of the Trinity. It's hard to define, but we can experience it!

Let me ask you something. If I gave you a pencil and paper right now and asked you to write your definition of the Trinity, what would you put down? The truth is that most of us would have difficulty, because this belief of "one God in three persons" is very confusing to many people. Let me show you what I mean.

Some years ago, Cardinal Cushing was walking through Macy's Department store in New York City. The manager of the store recognized the noted and famous Catholic priest and ran up to him, saying, "Cardinal Cushing! Come quickly! A man has passed out over here. He may have had a heart attack. He may be dying!" Let me hurry to say that the man had only fainted, and in a matter of just a very few minutes he would be perfectly okay. But Cardinal Cushing (not knowing that) rushed to the collapsed man, as any good priest would, knelt beside him, took his hand tenderly, and began to administer the last rites.

Cardinal Cushing said to the man, "My friend, do you believe in God the Father, God the Son, and God the Holy Spirit?" The man roused a little, opened one eye, looked at the people standing around and said, "Here I am dying, and he asks me a riddle!" For many people, the doctrine of the Trinity *is* a riddle: Father-Son-Holy Spirit? One plus one plus one equals one? One God in three persons? It does sound confusing and complex. What does it mean? How does it affect your life and mine?

Well, let me give you the key that will help unlock this theological puzzle, the key that will push back the heavy door of this belief and let us inside so that we can understand it better and celebrate it more. Here it is: The key is to remember that every doctrine was first a doxology—an expression of praise or thanksgiving— and that every belief was first a song! This means that we come to this belief not looking for what is here to argue about, but rather looking for what is here to sing about; not looking for what is here to squabble over, but instead looking for what is here that makes us want to shout and sing praises to God. The doctrine of the Trinity is like the concept of love. We don't have to worry about defining it, rather, we just experience it! We relish it, feel it, celebrate it.

Well, what's here to sing about? When we start at that point, the truth of the Trinity comes alive for us. We start with the fact that the early Christians were simply singing a hymn of praise to God for the three basic, dramatic ways in which they had experienced God as *Father-Creator*, as *Son-Savior,* and as *Holy Spirit-Sustainer.* Now, if you were to ask me how I have personally experienced God in my lifetime, I couldn't express it any better. God made me, God saved me, and God sustains me. Father-Son-Holy Spirit; one God, whom I have experienced in three distinct ways, as Creator-Savior-Sustainer. He makes us, he saves us, he sustains us.

Now, let's take a look at these three incredible doxologies.

FIRST, WE SING PRAISE TO THE FATHER-CREATOR

When the early Christians talked about God the Father, they were singing a majestic hymn of praise to the God who created us and who continues to provide for us. They were saying that God is the Maker of all things, the Lord of all life. But more, they were saying also that God loves his creation like a parent tenderly cares for his or her children.

One day in my searching, I ran across an idea that really spoke to me. It was first suggested by an English philosopher named William Paley, who lived about 200 years ago, and it goes something like this. Suppose you are walking across a field one day, when suddenly you see a watch on the ground. Imagine that you have never seen a watch before. You pick it up. You examine it. You see the hands moving in an orderly way. You open the watch and discover inside a host of wheels, cogs, springs, jewels, and levers, all ticking away. You notice that things are working together systematically and with purpose.

Now, what would you think? How would you size this up? Would you say, "Isn't this amazing, how all these things (the metal, the glass, the springs, the levers, the wheels) all fell together by chance, and by chance wound themselves up, and by chance made themselves into an instrument that keeps perfect time"? No! That's not what you would say at all. Rather, you would say, "I have found a watch. Somewhere there must be a watchmaker!"

So, when we find a universe that has an order more accurate, more purposeful, more dependable, and more systematic than we could even imagine, it is natural to say, "We have found a world. Somewhere there must be a world-maker!" Order implies mind. There must be a mind behind it all.

But there is more. God is not just a world-maker who winds her up and lets her go. No! God not only made us, he made us out of love, and for love. The incredible gift of God's loving creation has over the years prompted many hymn writers to write beautiful and powerful hymns of praise. For example, look at these words from the classic hymn "For the Beauty of the Earth."

> For the beauty of the earth,
> for the glory of the skies,
> for the love which from our birth

over and around us lies;
Lord of all, to thee we raise
this our hymn of grateful praise.

For the beauty of each hour
of the day and of the night,
hill and vale, and tree and flower,
sun and moon, and stars of light;
Lord of all, to thee we raise
this our hymn of grateful praise.

The God who made the universe created you and me. The God who created the world loves you and me. If you ever wonder about that, look at your fingerprints. Your fingerprints are unique—different from anybody else's who ever lived or ever will live. God put his distinct stamp of love on you and made you special, because you are special to him. If you still wonder about that, look at Jesus.

And that brings us to the second point. First, we sing praise to the Father-Creator.

SECOND, WE SING PRAISE TO THE SON-SAVIOR

There's a story about a little girl who was drawing a picture one day. Her mother walked by and asked her what she was drawing. Without looking up, the little girl answered confidently: "I'm drawing a picture of God." "But honey," her mother said, "How can you do that? Nobody knows what God looks like." The little girl replied, "Well, they will when I get through!"

Something like that happened with Jesus. He came painting God's picture, and they said to him, "Wait a minute, now! Nobody knows what God looks like." And Jesus said, in effect, "They will when I get through!" Jesus paints the portrait of God. He shows us what God is like and what God wants us to be like, and the word is *love!* God's incredible love not only *makes* us; it also *saves* us.

Have you heard the story about the man who had been known around town as a reprobate and a drunkard? But then Christ came into his life and saved him. Christ changed him completely and turned his life around. His coworkers noticed the change in him, and they tried to tease him, shake him, and challenge his faith. "Surely, you don't buy all that stuff in the Bible about miracles, do you?" they said to him. "Surely you don't really believe Jesus turned water into wine." "Whether he turned water into wine or not," said the man, "I don't know. I wasn't there. But I do know this: In my own house, I have seen him turn beer into furniture, whiskey into food, and tears into laughter!"

Now, I want to say something to you with all the feeling I have in my heart. I hope you become a great success, but listen. You can make a lot of money, you can rise to places of prominence in the world, you can have all the symbols of affluence; but if you don't have Christ in your heart as your personal Savior, your life will be an empty shell. Only those who learn how to live and love in the Spirit of Christ are truly successful! As Christians, we sing praise to the Father-Creator, and to the Son-Savior.

FINALLY, WE SING PRAISE TO THE HOLY SPIRIT-SUSTAINER

God makes us. God saves us. God also sustains us. He does not desert us. He does not leave us alone. He gives us his Holy Spirit to guide us, inspire us, strengthen us, comfort us, and encourage us.

Recently, I spent some time with an amazing family.

They have gone through so much trouble, disappointment, and heartache in the last few years, and yet they continue to inspire everyone who knows them with this incredible strength and courage. How do they do it? Well, many people have asked them that question. Their answer is always the same: "God is with us, and he will see us through." "God is with us"; that is the good news of our faith. From cover to cover, that is the message of the Bible: "God is with us."

Now, let me conclude with this, a dialogue between God and someone like you or me. Listen closely:

And the Lord said GO!
And I said who me?
And He said Yes You.
And I said
But I'm not ready yet
And there is studying to be done.
I've got this part-time job.
You know how tight my schedule is.
And He said You're Stalling.

Again the Lord said GO!
And I said I didn't want to.
And He said I Didn't Ask If You Wanted To.
And I said
Listen I'm not the kind of person to get involved in
   controversy.
Besides my friends won't like it
And what will my roommate think?
And He said Baloney.

And yet a third time the Lord said GO!
And I said do I have to?
And He said Do You Love Me?
And I said
Look I'm Scared.

People are going to hate me
And cut me into little pieces.
I can't take it all by myself.
And He said Where Do You Think I'll Be?

And the Lord said GO!
And I sighed
Here I am—send me.

That's what it's all about. Every doctrine was first a doxology. Every belief was first a song, a song of praise to God. So don't get lost in the questions and complexities. Just join in the song.

Praise be to the God who makes us, who saves us, who sustains us! Praise be to the Father, the Son, and the Holy Spirit!

11

Celebrating God's Gift of the Church
"I Was Glad When They Said to Me, 'Let Us Go to the House of the LORD!' "

Scripture: Psalm 122:1-9

Recently a good friend sent me an interesting e-mail message. It was entitled "Parenting 101: A Series of Tests on How You Can Know If You Are Ready to Have Children."

First, there is the Mess Test: Smear peanut butter on the sofa and curtains, rub wet mud from the flower beds on the wall, cover the stains with crayons, and place a fishstick behind the couch and leave it there all summer.

Next, there is the Toy Test: Buy a 55-gallon box of building blocks. Have a friend spread them on the floor all through the house. Then take off your shoes, put on a blindfold, and try to walk to the bathroom or kitchen without screaming.

Here is the Grocery Store Test: Borrow a few small animals (goats are best), and then take them with you as you shop at the grocery store. Always keep them in sight, and pay for anything they eat or damage.

Then there is the Dressing Test: Obtain one large, unhappy octopus. Try to stuff it into a small net bag, making sure all the arms stay inside.

Next is the Feeding Test: Obtain a large plastic milk jug. Fill it halfway with water and suspend it from the ceiling with a stout cord. Start the jug swinging back and forth, and then try to insert spoons full of soggy cereal into the mouth of the jug while pretending to be an airplane. When finished, dump the entire contents of the jug on the floor.

There is also the Night Test: Prepare by obtaining a small cloth bag and filling it with 8 to 12 pounds of sand. Soak it thoroughly in water. Put the bag down and set your alarm for 10:00 P.M. Get up at 10:00, pick up your bag, walk around the house with your bag, and sing every song you have ever heard and make up about a dozen more; sing these until 4:00 A.M. Lay the bag down. Set your alarm for 5:00 A.M. Get up and make breakfast. Keep this up for 5 years. Look cheerful.

Then there is the Physical Test for Women: Obtain a large beanbag. Attach to your front, under your clothes. Leave it there for 9 months. After the 9 months, remove 10 of the beans.

Here's the Physical Test for Men: Go to the nearest drugstore, set your wallet on the counter, and ask the clerk to help himself.

Now, the final test is the Lecture Test: Find a couple who already have a small child. Lecture them on how they can improve their discipline, their patience, their tolerance, and their child's table manners. Be firm. Enjoy this experience, because it will be the last time in your life that you will have all of the answers.

Parenting 101! It's interesting to me that when I first received this e-mail message with these humorous tests for child-readiness, my mind jumped to Christianity 101 and the tests for church-readiness, the tests for loyalty to our church, to our faith, and to our Christ. All of us who are members of the church, at some point in the past, stood at the altar of the church and took the test. We decided to accept Jesus Christ as our Lord and Savior, and we promised to love and support his church with our prayers, our presence, our gifts, and our service.

Just think of that. We stood at the altar of the church and promised God that we would support the church with our presence and make church attendance a priority in our lives. We would not waste energy each Sunday trying to decide, "Should I go to church today?" but decide now, once and for all, "I go to church. That's who I am. That's what I do. That's a number-one priority in my life. I made that promise to God, and I'm going to honor that promise."

Last week I was reading a story in Fred Craddock's book *Craddock Stories*. This story touched me because it reminded me of something from my early childhood. Fred Craddock, one of the great preachers and teachers in America today, told about a time when he, along with some other ministers and teachers, was asked to tell a large audience who was the most influential person in the formation of his life, not counting his parents or Jesus. He had two or three weeks to think about this. Finally, when the big event came, Dr. Craddock stood and gave them an unfamiliar name: Miss Emma Sloan.

Miss Emma had been Fred's Sunday school teacher when he was a child. She taught him every Sunday for several years. One year she gave Fred Craddock a Bible. She wrote in the front these words: *"May this be a light to your feet, a lamp to your path. Emma Sloan."*

She taught Fred and the other children to memorize great Bible verses. She said, "Just put it in your heart. Just put it in your heart, and it will serve you well all your days." Miss Emma used the alphabet, and students would take turns responding. She would point to a student and say "A," and the student would quote a verse that began with the letter A. It went like this:

A—"A soft answer turns away wrath."

B—"Be kind to one another."

C—"Come unto me all you who are heavy laden, and I will give you rest."

D—"Do unto others as you would have them do unto you."

E—"Every good and perfect gift."

F—"For God so loved the world He gave His only son."

Don't worry now; I'm not going to do the whole alphabet! But you ought to try that sometime. Dr. Craddock said, "What an incredible influence Miss Emma was on my life!" He said, "I still remember all of that. I can't think of anything, anything in all my life, that has made such a radical difference as those verses. The Spirit of God brings them to my mind appropriately, time and time and time again" ([St. Louis: Chalice Press, 2001], pp. 33-34).

Now, the reason Fred Craddock's story reminded me of my childhood was because I had a Sunday school teacher who did that with us. Her name was Miss Frances, and I would always try to get in the ninth or tenth position in the order of participants, because I had figured out that then I would get *I* or *J*. I always remembered two verses, and they started with *I* and *J*. The *J* verse was "Jesus wept" (John 11:35 RSV). I could always remember that. I learned later that that poignant verse has indeed a powerful message and meaning, but as an eight-year-old boy I liked it because it was short and I could always remember it.

The one letter-*I* verse that I could always remember is

from the Scripture for this chapter: "I was glad when they said unto me, Let us go into the house of the Lord" (Psalm 122:1 KJV). When I would quote that verse in class, Miss Frances would always smile warmly, because she had this great love for the church. Being in the church was joy and gladness for her. You could see it in her face.

And like Dr. Craddock, I have to tell you that those Bible verses I learned as an eight-year-old child have served me well over the years. They have been a constant source of strength and comfort and inspiration and wisdom. I still love that verse: "I was glad when they said to me, 'Let us go to the house of the Lord.'"

I love that verse because it rings so true for me. It is genuine joy and gladness for me to be in the church. I'm sure this is one of the main reasons I heard the call of God to come into the ministry. All of my life (for as long as I can remember), I have loved being in the church. I love the feel of the church, the message of the church, the music of the church, the theology of the church, the outreach of the church, the love and support of the church, and the Christian spirit of the church.

As we know, life in today's world can be tough, hard, and scary. Life can be so challenging and so demanding and so draining. The church is the place; it's the community of love; it's where we get our spiritual batteries recharged. I don't know about you, but I need that every week. Let me show you why with three reasons—three special ways in which the church recharges our spiritual batteries.

FIRST, IT REMINDS US OF HOW MUCH GOD LOVES US

When Jesus got ready to say the best thing he could think of to say about God, do you remember what he said? He did not say that God is an angry judge who is out to get us. He did not say that God is an impersonal computer, automatically rewarding us when we do good and punishing us when we do bad. No! He said that God is a loving parent who loves us more than we can imagine, more than words could ever describe.

When our daughter, Jodi (our firstborn), went away to college, we talked to her on the phone every day. We still do, and I don't mind that big phone bill one bit. When she went away to college, we would go over on Saturday afternoons for the football games, and we would take our binoculars. Jodi would sit in the student section with thousands of other students, and we would sit with the parents on the other side of the field. And do you know what we would do, first thing? We would take those high-powered binoculars, scan the student section, and focus in on Jodi, not to spy on her, but because she was our daughter, gone away to college for the first time. We would watch the game and enjoy the pageantry of college football on a Saturday afternoon, but most of all, we would focus in on Jodi, because she is our daughter and we love her more than you can imagine. The first time we did this (she knows us so well!), when we finally spotted her in that sea of thousands of faces, she and four of her friends were standing up and looking back at us through their binoculars, waving and laughing and holding up a sign that read "Yes, Mom and Dad, we know you are watching!"

One time we went to the game and the governor was there, a senator was there, a congressman was there, Miss America was there, former pro quarterback Terry Bradshaw was there; and they are all fine, and we looked at them. But most of all, we were focused on Jodi, our daughter. A few years later she became a cheerleader, and it was easier to spot her then. And when our son, Jeff, came along and played football, we would go to the games, and we had the binoculars on him during every play, because he is our son. Our eyes never left our children.

Now, let me tell you something: That's the way God loves you—like a loving parent. Sometimes in the rough and tumble of life we forget that, and that's why we need to come to church every Sunday, to get our spiritual batteries recharged with this amazing, incredible message of how much God loves us.

SECOND, GOING TO CHURCH RECHARGES OUR SPIRITUAL BATTERIES BECAUSE IT REMINDS US OF THE IMPORTANCE OF PRACTICING THE HOLY HABITS

A couple of years ago, Tom Tewell, pastor of Fifth Avenue Presbyterian Church in New York, was asked to lead a retreat in Malibu, in Southern California, in February. Tom said it was tough work but somebody had to do it! While there, they had a free Saturday afternoon, and some of the folks at the retreat took Tom to see the Los Angeles Open golf tournament. Tiger Woods and Phil Mickelson were leading the tournament. Tom and his friends watched Tiger Woods play, and it was a phenomenal experience. But Tom said what was more phenomenal was to watch what Tiger Woods did after his round. He went with his golf instructor to the driving range (the practice tee) and hit 5-iron after 5-iron after 5-iron. For thirty minutes Tom and his friends watched Tiger Woods work on his 5-iron shots. Every so often the instructor would walk over and adjust his grip, and then Tiger Woods would hit 5-iron after 5-iron after

5-iron, with perfect precision. Even his divots were perfect.

Then Tom and his friends went back out on the course and watched Phil Mickelson and David Duval play. Two hours later they came back by the practice tee, and what do you think they saw? Tiger Woods, still hitting 5-iron after 5-iron after 5-iron.

Now, there's a sermon here somewhere, and let me tell you what it is. The next day on the 18th hole, Tiger Woods and Phil Mickelson were still tied for the lead. Tiger needed a birdie to win. He hit a drive that went way off to the left, almost out of bounds. He was 213 yards away from the green, and he had a very difficult second shot to play. He reached into his golf bag and pulled out—his 5-iron! Tiger Woods hit that 5-iron. The ball landed just a few feet from the hole. He made his birdie putt and won the tournament!

Now, here's the sermon. Tiger Woods was prepared to hit the shot because he had practiced, practiced, practiced. Over and over and over again, he had hit that shot. He had listened to lessons from his instructor, and over and over and over, he had hit that shot. You see, you never know when you are going to need that 5-iron shot. You've got to have it ready. You don't learn it in the moment of crisis. You've got to have it with you at all times.

So, what does this mean for you and me? Simply this: You want a good prayer life? Here's how you do it: 5-iron, 5-iron, 5-iron—or in other words, *practice, practice, practice!* You want to have a good understanding of the Scriptures? Here's how you do it: 5-iron, 5-iron, 5-iron—or in other words, *practice, practice, practice!* You want to be a good church member? Here's how you do it: 5-iron,

5-iron, 5-iron! You want strength of character and love for others and devoted service to God? Here's how you do it: 5-iron, 5-iron, 5-iron!

Coming to church regularly, every Sunday, recharges our spiritual batteries. Because first of all, it reminds us of how much God loves us; and second, it reminds us of the importance of practicing the Holy Habits, like prayer, Bible study, and corporate worship.

THIRD AND FINALLY, GOING TO CHURCH RECHARGES OUR SPIRITUAL BATTERIES BECAUSE IT REMINDS US OF THE POWER OF JESUS

You want to know what's special about the church? I'll tell you in one word: *Jesus*. In our hectic world, we can so easily become the victims of what Marshall McLuhan called "implosion," all kinds of ideas and causes and philosophies flooding in on us and vying for our attention, energy, loyalty, and resources. What do we believe? Where do we put our weight down? What do we give our heart to? In whom can we put our trust?

Well, we have the answer. We've had it all along. We've had it for over 2,000 years. It's in the Book. Jesus Christ is the answer—yesterday, today, tomorrow, and forever. So don't be taken in by all of these exotic, high-sounding fads that come along screaming for our allegiance. Just come to church and give your heart and soul to Jesus.

Now, let me tell you something I did in church one Sunday morning. I asked the congregation a series of questions and asked them to answer out loud.

First, I said, "On the count of three, say out loud the name of the town where you were born." They did, and it was total chaos.

Then, I said, "On the count of three, say out loud the name of the month in which you were born." They answered, and again it was confusion like that at the Tower of Babel.

Then, I said, "On the count of three, say out loud the name of your favorite color." Again they responded all at once, with a variety of answers.

Next, I said, "On the count of three, say out loud the name of your favorite sport." Again, there was a loud noise of indistinguishable sounds.

But then, finally, I said, "On the count of three, say out loud the first name of your Savior." It was amazing. Clear as a bell, in perfect unison, they all said, "Jesus!"

The point is clear. Some of us like football and others like baseball or basketball or golf. Some of us like blue, some red, some yellow, and some purple. Some of us were born in April and some in May. But the one thing we share in common, the one thing that unites us, the one thing that makes us a church, the One who saves us is *Jesus!*

He is the hope of the world, and he is your best friend. There is nothing that will charge your spiritual batteries more than knowing that. And the best place to find that out is in church, Sunday after Sunday after Sunday.

12

Celebrating God's Gift of Freedom

Made for the Skies and Crammed in a Cage

Scripture: Romans 12:1-2

The great British minister Dr. W. E. Sangster once told about the day he went to the zoo. He was walking about, seeing the sights, and he came upon an eagle in a cage. He looked at that eagle. He saw those amazingly powerful wings, those beautifully feathered wings, meant for the skies, meant for flying.

As he stood there looking at that eagle in captivity, someone in the crowd said aloud exactly what Dr. Sangster was feeling. Someone looked at that magnificent eagle housed in that small pen, and said, "Made for the skies and crammed in a cage."

Think about that phrase for a moment: "Made for the skies and crammed in a cage." There's a sermon there somewhere. That phrase brings many different images to my mind. I think of the apostle Paul, in our Scripture for this chapter, writing to the Christians in Rome and saying, "Don't let the world around you squeeze you into its own [mold]" (Romans 12:2 J. B. Phillips). Isn't that just another way of saying, "You are made for the skies, so don't let the world cram you into a cage"?

Also, I think of Søren Kierkegaard, the noted and respected Danish theologian, and his story about the wild duck flying south for the winter. The duck looked down and saw an abundant supply of corn in a barn-yard, so it swooped down, took a closer look, and decided to spend the winter eating corn in that barn-yard. Then in the spring, when the other wild ducks flew over heading north, the wild duck tried to fly up and join his friends, but he couldn't get off the ground—he had become too fat, too tame, too domesti-cated. So he remained trapped in the boredom of the barnyard, imprisoned by his own greed and laziness. That wild duck was made for the skies, but he was crammed into a cage of his own making.

Then too, I think of Harry Emerson Fosdick, the famous pastor of Riverside Church in New York City, and his fascinating story about a vulture. It was a win-try day on the Niagara River, below Buffalo, New York. The vulture, this bird of prey, lighted on a carcass float-ing down the river and began to feed. It intended to feed as long as it could, and then at the last moment to fly away to safety just above the falls. But when the time came, the vulture tried to fly away only to dis-cover to its horror that its claws had become frozen to the carcass it was feeding on. And the vulture plunged over the falls to its death. That vulture was made for the skies, but it was crammed into a cage of its own making, imprisoned and destroyed by the clutch of its claws.

Like the vulture, our hands freeze to that which we feed upon, and though we are meant for the skies, we are crammed into a cage.

If we are self-centered, we are crammed into the cage of selfishness.

If we feed on defeat, we are crammed into the cage of negativism.

If we are hooked on alcohol or drugs or tranquilizers, we are crammed into the cage of escapism.

If we always maintain the status quo, we are crammed into the cage of the closed mind.

If we are jealous or resentful, we are crammed into the cage of hate.

If we constantly talk badly about other people, we are crammed into the cage of gossip.

If we are anxiety-ridden, we are crammed into the cage of fear.

If we are frozen in one of those debilitating attitudes, we are headed for a fall! We have lost our freedom! We are made for the skies, but we have been crammed into a cage.

Have you ever noticed that many people let one little thing eclipse their lives and enslave them—something like prejudice or envy or a bad temper or a worried spirit or nervous tension or hostility? What about you? Is there anything in your life that's making a slave of you? You were made for the skies. You were meant for greatness. But are you letting stubborn pride or selfishness or closed-mindedness or hate or jealousy or apathy cram you into a cage?

It's something to think about, isn't it? So, with these thoughts as a backdrop and with Paul's warning, "Don't let the world around you squeeze you into its own [mold]," ringing in our ears, let's look together at three devastating attitudes that can absolutely imprison us. At first glance, these three attitudes don't seem so bad or so dangerous, but they can immobilize us, and they can imprison us probably much more dramatically than we realize.

FIRST, THERE IS SELF-PITY

Self-pity, ingratitude, complaining, grumbling, whining—whatever you want to call it, one thing is for sure, it's a terrible cage to live in.

The noted and respected writer Maya Angelou has written a beautiful piece about this that makes the point well. She reminisces about growing up in Stamps, Arkansas, and the great, invaluable lesson she learned from her grandmother.

Maya Angelou's grandmother was well educated in the school of "hard knocks" and was exceptionally wise in the ways of the world. She had a special way of getting right to the heart of the matter.

Maya Angelou's grandmother didn't care for the whiners of the world and didn't want Maya to become a whiner or complainer, so she would teach Maya through graphic life examples how bad it sounds to whine and gripe and complain.

When people would come into her store whom she knew to be whiners, she would signal compiratorially to Maya to watch and listen. While the loud, pitiful lamentations of complaints would fill the room, Maya's grandmother would stand there stoically and listen to the unending griping and groaning, occasionally saying, "Uh huh, uh huh," and cutting her eyes toward Maya with a look that said, "Maya, are you listening to this? Are you hearing how that sounds?"

When the complainer would finish and leave the store, Maya's grandmother would turn to Maya and give her the lesson—a lesson Maya said she heard from her grandmother again and again. "Maya, did you hear that? Did you hear how awful that whining and com-

120

plaining sounds? Did you see how pitiful that kind of attitude is?"

Maya would nod and her grandmother would sum it all up with these words:

> There are people who went to sleep all over the world last night, poor and rich and white and black, but they will never wake again. Sister, those who expected to rise did not, their beds became their cooling boards and their blankets became their winding sheets. And those dead folks would give anything, anything at all for just five minutes of this weather or ten minutes of that plowing that person was grumbling about. So, you watch yourself about complaining, Sister. What you're supposed to do when you don't like a thing is change it. If you can't change it, change the way you think about it. Don't complain." (*Wouldn't Take Nothing for My Journey Now* [New York: Random House, 1993], pp. 85-87)

Maya Angelou's grandmother was right, wasn't she? She was saying the same thing that Jesus had said so many years before:

Don't feel so sorry for yourself.

Don't be so fretful.

Don't be so anxious.

Don't be so ungrateful.

Don't be so self-centered.

Don't give in to whining and complaining and griping and grumbling.

Don't give in to self-pity.

Don't get crammed into that cage; it will imprison you.

In his book, *Keeping First Things First,* John Gile put it like this (page 75): "Look out for self-pity. It is one of the most overlooked, powerful, devastating, clever, insidious forms of evil—because it is not recognized as evil. It gets past our guard, distorts reality, and provokes anger. Self-pity takes away our sense of humor, shuts down communication, and stifles our creative power. It makes us concentrate on ourselves, miss the good we could be doing for others, and blocks out the voice of God. Letting all that happen to us is what makes self-pity so pitiful."

That's number one—the prison of self-pity. Don't get crammed into that cage.

SECOND, THERE IS RESENTMENT

Some years ago in Australia, a man came up with what he thought was a most creative plan to escape from the county jail. Here's what he did. He crawled under a delivery truck parked inside the prison at the receiving dock. He held on for dear life to the underpinnings of the truck as it passed through the prison gates and then proceeded out and down the main highway.

Twenty minutes later, the truck began to slow down. When it came to a complete stop, the prisoner let go of his grip, dropped to the ground, and rolled out to freedom. At least that's what he meant to do. Actually what happened was this: As he rolled out from under the truck, he discovered that he was now inside the walls of the state prison, five miles from the county jail from whence he had come. His attempt to escape one prison had simply landed him in another one.

That's what the prison of resentment does to us. It incarcerates us everywhere we go. It taints everything we do. It poisons every relationship.

I know a man who lives daily in the prison of resentment. He is angry at everybody.

He's mad at the President.
He's mad at the Congress.
He's mad at the Senate.
He's mad at the mayor.
He's mad at his neighbors.
He's mad at his children.
He's mad at God.
He's mad at everybody.
He's mad at life.

Like that prisoner in Australia, he just goes from one "mad" to another.

And do you know what? He didn't used to be that way. I remember when he was a happy, productive, nice, friendly guy who was fun to be around. But no more. Now, he lives daily in the prison of resentment. You just dread to see him coming because you know he's going to be angry about something, and he's going to take it all out on you.

Why? How did this happen? How did he get crammed into the cage of resentment? Well, let me tell you the story.

He had a lovely wife. She was so devoted to him. She helped him and supported him in every way, and over their forty-something years of marriage, she only asked him for one thing: She wanted them to go on a cruise. Now, he meant to take her, but he was so busy in his responsible job. He put her off and put her off and put her off, and finally, he said, "As soon as I retire, we will go on that cruise." But there was one thing he didn't count on. Two days after his retirement dinner, she had a massive stroke, and subsequently died. Of course, he never took her on that cruise. And now, he has moved into the prison of resentment—mad at everybody, mad at everything, mad at life, but really, mad at himself.

First, there is the prison of self-pity. Second, there is the prison of resentment. God never meant for us to live like that. God made us for the skies, so don't get crammed into those cages.

THIRD AND FINALLY, THERE IS THE RUSH TO SUCCESS

"The Rat Race," "The Rush to Success," "Becoming Number One at Any Cost," "Always Trying to Get Ahead," or whatever you want to call it, one thing is for sure: It's a terrible cage to live in. Let me show you what I mean.

After returning home from yet another stress-filled, pressure-packed, intensely busy, and highly aggravating day, a young businessman slumped into his easy chair to read the paper and to try to relax. His curious little eight-year-old son approached. "Daddy, how much do you get paid per hour?" Irritated and annoyed by the question, the father snapped, "I don't know, Billy—twenty dollars or so, I guess. Why are you asking me questions like that? Can't you see I'm tired?"

"I'm sorry, Daddy," the little boy said, and he ran out of the room. In a while, Billy was back with another question: "Daddy, can I borrow seven dollars and fifty-five cents?" This time, the young father really got aggravated, and he snapped, "Billy, this is ridiculous! It's nighttime. You don't need money now. Just go to your room right now. I'm not in the mood for your games tonight!"

A while later, the father felt guilty for being so rough on little Billy. He went to his son's room to check on him. "Billy, I'm sorry I was so short with you earlier. I guess I had a bad day at the office. Sure, I'll loan you the money. Here it is—seven dollars and fifty-five cents. But tell me, what do you need it for?"

Billy's eyes widened. He reached under his pillow and pulled out a box, which contained some one-dollar bills and some coins. "Thanks, Dad, this is great! Now I have enough!" "Enough for what, Son?" asked the father. "Enough to buy an hour of your time, Dad" (Paul Harvey, *The Rest of the Story* broadcast).

The prison of self-pity, the prison of resentment, the prison of the rush to succeed—God never meant for us to live like that. God never meant for us to be crammed into those cages or squeezed into those molds. And God is the One, the only One, who can set us free.

There's a powerful line in the movie entitled *The Hurricane*. Denzel Washington plays the part of Hurricane Carter, a well-known professional boxer who spent years in prison for a crime he did not commit. Hurricane Carter speaks through prison bars to a young boy who is convinced that Hurricane Carter is innocent and who is working to get him set free. Hurricane Carter (Denzel Washington) says to the boy: "Hate put me in prison. Love's gonna bust me out."

I don't know what prison you may be in right now. Maybe it's guilt or fear or pride or anger. Maybe it's self-pity or resentment or the rush to success. I don't know what is imprisoning you right now, but I do know this: God's love in Jesus Christ can bust you out.

13

Celebrating the Spirit of Christ

Whom Do You Trust?

Scripture: John 13:34-35

My wife, June, has a sister named Dale who lives in Milan, Tennessee. Dale and her husband, Gary, and their daughter, Ashley, have a nice home that is located near a beautiful wooded area in Milan. Recently, Dale came home from work, weary from a long, hard day. She put her glasses on the kitchen table and then went out onto the patio to feed the family cat.

A beautiful sunset was in the making, so Dale quickly filled the cat's feeding dish and sat down in a lawn chair on the patio to rest, to wind down from the day, and to enjoy the gorgeous colors of the Tennessee sky at sunset. The cat ran up, ate the cat food, and, as cats will do, went over and began rubbing affectionately against Dale's legs and ankles. Dale, still savoring the sunset, reached down to pet and stroke the cat. This went on for several minutes—just Dale, enjoying the peace and quiet and beauty, and tenderly petting the family cat.

But then, Dale's husband, Gary, very gently opened the patio door from inside the house, and almost in a whisper, he said, "Dale, don't make any sudden moves. Don't turn around. Just listen to me and quietly answer this question:

"Do you trust me? . . ."

"Yes, of course I trust you," Dale answered.

"Okay, then," Gary said, "here's what I want you to do. With no questions asked, very gently, very quietly, just stand up and walk slowly into the house."

Dale didn't have any idea what was going on, but she trusted Gary, so she followed his instructions perfectly. She gently stood up and slowly walked into the house and closed the sliding glass door behind her; and she said, "What in the world was that all about? I was just sitting out there enjoying the sunset and petting the cat." To which Gary replied, "Well, I just wanted you to see what you were petting." Dale looked out the sliding glass door and saw to her amazement that what she had been petting was not the family cat; it was a skunk!

The point is clear and obvious. Dale was saved from (how shall I put this?) an unpleasant and unfragrant experience simply because she trusted her husband. She didn't know at the moment what was going on. She didn't know at the moment why he was telling her to do those things. She didn't know at the moment why it all seemed so urgent to him. But she did know that Gary had her best interest at heart, and so she trusted him. And it was a good thing she did! It raises an interesting question, doesn't it? Namely this: Whom do you trust? It is one of the single most critical questions of life. In whom or in what do you put your trust?

Everywhere we go, every step we take, there is an incessant clamoring for our trust. From every corner, they are screaming in our ears loudly, or whispering in our ears temptingly, "Put your trust in me." "Put your hope in me." "Give your allegiance to me." "You can count on me." Money says that. Military might says that. Gangs and cliques say that. Alcohol and drugs say that. Material things say that. They all say, enticingly, "Put your trust in me. Put your hope in me. Give your allegiance to me."

I can't stop thinking about the tragedy of September 11, 2001. Those men who crashed those planes into the World Trade Center and the Pentagon had put their trust in violence and assault, in anger and rage and prejudice and revenge—*and it didn't work*. It didn't work! And the result was death, destruction, suffering, heartache, and incredible loss for so many. Indescribable, horrific pain for so many because those men put their trust in the wrong things. Unbelievable agony for so many because those men chose wrongly. Who and what we trust is so crucial!

One of my favorite passages in all of Scripture is found in John 13:34-35. Jesus knew that the cross loomed near, and he was trying to get his disciples ready to take up the torch of his ministry. He said to them: "I give you a new commandment, that you love one another. Just as I have loved you, you also should love one another. By this everyone will know that you are my disciples."

Notice that Jesus didn't just say "Love one another." He said to love one another "just as I have loved you." He was saying to them, "Take on my spirit, see things as I see them, care for people as I have cared for them. Don't put your trust in selfishness; put your trust in self-giving love."

The lesson for now is obvious: Put your trust in him! Put your trust in the spirit of Christ, because when you look at life through the eyes of Christ, you forget about yourself, and everywhere you look, you will see people to help, problems to solve, and opportunities to serve. Let's take a look at each of these.

FIRST OF ALL, WHEN WE LIVE IN THE SPIRIT OF CHRIST, EVERYWHERE WE LOOK WE SEE PEOPLE TO HELP

Nothing was more characteristic of Jesus than that. He could always see people to help, and he could always see how to help them. Just think of that.

Think of the man who had been unable to walk for thirty-eight years; no one else noticed him anymore. He had been there for so long that he was, for most people, just a part of the landscape. But not so to Jesus! Jesus saw him and helped him.

Or, think of—

The woman in the crowd with the flow of blood (Luke 8:43-48).

The man who had been blind from birth (John 9:1-41).

The ten lepers (Luke 17:11-19).

Bartimaeus by the side of the road (Mark 10:46-52).

Zacchaeus up in a tree (Luke 19:1-10).

No one else paid any attention to them, didn't see them. But not so with Jesus. He was so good at that. His mind was tuned in to that. He could always see people to help.

If Jesus came into your sanctuary next Sunday to share in your worship experience, where do you think he would sit? I think he would see immediately the person who is hurting the most today, and I think he would slip in and sit by that person and meet that person's need. His mind was so finely tuned to sense and see people to help.

Some years ago, there was a little boy who came from a poor family. One summer, though he was very young, he took a job as a door-to-door salesman to help make money to buy his school supplies. One afternoon he was so hungry. He had been working all day, hadn't had anything to eat, and he only had one dime in his pocket. He decided that he would ask for a meal at the next house. However, he lost his nerve when a lovely young woman opened the door. Instead of a meal, he asked for a drink of water. She thought he looked hungry, so she brought him four large cookies and a glass of milk. He enjoyed it all so much, and then he said, "How much do I owe you?" "You don't owe me anything," she replied. "Mother taught us long ago to never accept pay for a kindness." He said, "Then I thank you from my heart."

As young Howard Kelly left that house, he not only felt stronger physically, but his faith in God and his love for people were made strong again. He had been so discouraged that he had been about ready to give up and quit on life.

Years later, that kind woman became critically ill. The local doctors were baffled, so they sent her to the large medical center in the nearby big city. Medical specialists were brought in to study her rare disease. One of the doctors was Dr. Howard Kelly. When he heard that the patient was from his small hometown, he went down to the room to see if he might recognize her. He realized at once that this was the woman who had been so kind to him so many years ago. He immediately volunteered to take her case, and after a long struggle, the battle was won. Her life was saved.

She was so thankful, but she wondered how in the world she would ever pay the huge medical bill. Dr. Kelly came to her room to tell her good-bye on the day that she was to go home. After a brief visit, he handed her a white envelope. It was the bill. With trembling hands, she opened it. She looked at the bottom line. She blinked and looked again. She couldn't believe her eyes. It read

Amount owed by patient: $0.00

She looked up at Dr. Howard Kelly. "I don't understand," she said. He replied, "Read the PS." She read it aloud: "A beautiful young woman taught me years ago to never accept payment for a kindness, but if you need a bill for your records, here it is: 'Paid in full with four large cookies and a glass of milk.' "

"You mean," she said, *"you* were that little boy?"

"Yes," he said, "and you saw that I needed help that afternoon. You saw how hungry I was—and your kindness restored my faith and turned my life around."

At that moment, somewhere in heaven, God was smiling, because nothing makes the heart of God happier than when people take on the spirit of Christ, see people to help, and reach out in kindness to help them.

As Christians, who do we trust? We trust the spirit of Christ, and we commit ourselves to living in that spirit. And when we do, everywhere we go, we see people to help.

SECOND, WHEN WE LIVE IN THE SPIRIT OF CHRIST, EVERYWHERE WE LOOK WE SEE PROBLEMS TO SOLVE

Some years ago, there was a man who lived in Scotland named Joseph Craik. He became a legend in his own time. He was known all over Scotland as "the man who turned inkblots into angels." Joseph Craik was a talented and creative teacher of penmanship. He was the writing master in a village school in Scotland. Often, as children will do when they are learning, his young students would leave inkblots on their pages. While most teachers would chastise the students for leaving inkblots on their work, circling them in red and taking away points for sloppy penmanship, Joseph Craik would do something quite different and delightful. Joseph Craik would take his pen in his talented hand, and beginning with the blots made by the children, he would add a line here and another one there, and out of the inkblots, he would draw pictures of angels! So, when the students received their papers back, they weren't all marked up with harsh criticisms. Rather, they were wonderfully decorated with exquisite angels! The children were delighted, pleased, and encouraged, and Joseph Craik became known far and wide as the man who turned inkblots into angels.

This is a great parable for the Christian faith. By the miracle of his grace, God can take the problems, the inkblots of our lives, and turn them into angels. God can take our feeble efforts and use them. God can take our mistakes and redeem them. God can take our heartaches and heal them.

This is also a great parable for Christian living. As we take on the spirit of Christ, we can see problems to solve, and we can trust God to help us.

Remember what a great problem-solver Jesus was.

He saw a wedding feast hostess about to be embarrassed, and he stepped up and solved the problem (John 2:1-11).

He saw his disciples causing a ruckus because some mothers wanted their children to see him up close, and he stepped in and solved the problem (Matthew 19:13-15).

Fishermen having no luck catching fish, folks being bilked out of money in the Temple, a huge throng of people hungry on a hillside—whatever the problem, Jesus knew how to size it up and solve it. He knew how to turn defeats into victories. And he always did it in the spirit of love and compassion.

That's our calling, isn't it—to put our trust in the mind of Christ and see people to help, and problems to solve.

THIRD AND FINALLY, WHEN WE LIVE IN THE SPIRIT OF CHRIST, EVERYWHERE WE LOOK WE SEE OPPORTUNITIES TO SERVE

A successful young executive was proudly driving his new Jaguar a bit too fast down a neighborhood street. He slowed just a bit as he passed some parked cars. Suddenly, there was a *thump* against the side of his car. Someone had hit his car with a brick. He was furious. He backed up, jumped out, ran between the cars, grabbed a young boy, and shouted at him, "What was that all about? Why did you throw that brick at my car? That's a brand-new car, and it's going to take a lot of money to fix it!"

The young boy started to cry. "I'm sorry, Mister. I didn't know what else to do. I threw the brick because I couldn't get anybody to stop." He pointed to a spot just around the parked car. "It's my brother. He rolled off the curb and fell out of his wheelchair, and I can't lift him up. Would you please help me get him back into his wheelchair? He's hurt, and he's too heavy for me."

The young executive swallowed the lump in his throat, rushed over to the boy, helped him back into his chair, looked him over quickly, and saw that he was okay. "Thank you, and may God bless you," said the grateful boy. The man stood there in silence and watched the boy push his brother down the sidewalk and toward their home. Then the young executive walked back to his Jaguar. The dent made by the brick was noticeable, but he never got it repaired. He kept the dent there to remind him of this message: *Don't go through life so fast that someone has to throw a brick at you to get your attention.*

Can you relate to that story? Can you? Are you rushing through life so fast that you are unable to see people to help, problems to solve, and opportunities to serve? If so, it's time to slow down and take on the spirit of Christ. Put your trust in God for the future, and put your trust in the spirit of Christ for the living of these days.

14

Celebrating God's Blueprint for Life

A Formula for Living

Scripture: Philippians 2:12-13

T he noted author Robert Fulghum was seated next to a young woman in an airport in Hong Kong. He noted that her backpack "bore the scars and dirt of some hard traveling, and it bulged with mysterious souvenirs of seeing the world." He could not help noticing, however, that big tears were streaming down her cheeks. He imagined a love left behind or the sorrow of leaving a great adventure only to have to return to school.

Before long, her gentle tears turned into a veritable flood, and she was now sobbing loudly. Through her sobbing she told him that she had run out of money and had to go home sooner than she had wanted. She had spent the entirety of the last two days waiting in the airport on standby, with no money, nothing to eat. But what was really upsetting her now was the fact that after all this time, she finally had gotten a seat on the next plane out, but she could not find her ticket, and the plane was about to take off. She had been sitting in this one spot for three hours, hungry, tired, frustrated, distressed, and depressed.

Robert Fulghum was joined by an older couple from Illinois. They dried the young woman's tears and hugged her, invited her to a meal, and offered to talk to "the powers that be" at the airline about replacing her ticket. Relieved at this help, she stood up and turned around to pick up her things, and with that, let out a loud scream. Thinking something terrible had happened to her, Robert Fulghum and the older couple rushed over to her, only to discover that her scream was not one of agony but rather joy. She had found her lost tickets! Apparently, she had been sitting on them for three hours (*It Was on Fire When I Lay Down on It* [New York: Villard Books, 1989], pp. 197-99).

Now, that true story from the airport in Hong Kong is a fascinating parable for us today, because the truth is that many people go through life like that, "sitting on their tickets"! That is, they wallow in self-pity, they think everybody's against them, they throw in the towel, they sink into deep despair, they get angry and frustrated, and they just give up and quit on life. They think they've lost their tickets, but really they're just sitting on them. The solution is right there with them. The answer is right there within easy reach. It has been there all along.

This is what the apostle Paul was talking about when he said to the Philippians, in effect, "Now, I'm not going to be around much longer to spoon-feed you, so you need to work out your own salvation; that is to say, Grow up! Stand tall! Be strong! Be mature! Take responsibility now for your own life and faith and morality. God will be there for you every step of the way. He will see you through. He has bought your tickets at a great price, and he has given you an unbeatable formula for living."

As was mentioned in chapter 5, the Bible is so important for us because it contains the blueprint, the formula, for building the kind of life God wants us to build. It is the key to our fulfillment, the key to making life work. What is that unbeatable formula for living? What is our faith? How can we express it clearly and concisely? Perhaps like this. As you go out into the world, remember these three things:

Life is worth living;

People are worth loving; and

Christ is worth following.

Let's take a look at these together.

FIRST OF ALL, LIFE IS WORTH LIVING

I know that life can be hard. I know it can be tough. Leonard Sweet tells about a deep-sea diver who was walking on the ocean floor one day, hooked up by an air hose and a speaker system to the ship on the surface. All of a sudden he heard a frantic voice coming through his sound system: "Come up, quick! The ship is sinking!" There's a message there somewhere! But let me ask you: *Is* the ship sinking? No, it's not sinking, but we will all have days when we think it is. We will all have days when we will readily agree with the little orphan girls in the Broadway musical *Annie,* "It's a Hard-Knock Life!" And yet, I am convinced with all my heart that life is good, that life is a miracle, and that life is a precious and sacred gift from God. Someone once said, "Life is God's gift to us; what we do with it is our gift back to him."

I want to put a picture-image into your minds that I hope you will never forget. Here it is.

A woman came to her doctor yet again. She came to him a lot, and once again she said the same thing. "Doctor, I feel blue and depressed and sad today. Give me something that will make me happy."

The doctor answered, "Come back here. I want to

show you something." He took her back into one of the supply rooms where there were rows and rows and rows of empty medicine bottles, and he said, "Do you see these bottles? They are all empty now. Empty bottles just waiting to be filled. I have to make a choice about what to put into them. I can either put in poison that will kill or I can put in medicine that will heal. The choice is mine."

He paused for a moment to let that sink in, and then he said, "You know, our days on this earth are like those empty bottles, and the question we face daily is, What am I going to put into the bottle called *today*? Will it be poison that will devastate and destroy and kill? Or will it be good medicine that will bring hope and life and healing? The choice is ours each day."

If we are followers of the Great Physician, the choice is clear. With the help of God we can say, "This is the day the Lord has made; I will rejoice and be glad in it." With the help of God, we can say yes to life. With the help of God, we can say that life is good, life is a miracle, life is a precious and sacred gift from God. With the help of God, we can say that life is worth living.

That's number one.

SECOND, PEOPLE ARE WORTH LOVING

Over and over, Jesus taught us that. More than anything else, he urged us to love people.

Some years ago, a beautiful older woman in our church family died. She had lived a wonderful life for many years, deeply committed to Christ and his church, so loving toward her family and friends, and really toward everybody she met. I went to her son's home to help the family through their grief experience and to plan the funeral.

We worked out all of the details for a memorial service that would be just the right tribute to this lovely lady, and then we began to reminisce about the special qualities of her life. We talked about her zest for living and her sense of humor, her love for this city and for our church, her devotion to her family and friends, her deep Christian spirit, and then, as almost on cue, they all said, "Roses! She loved red roses."

I suggested that they might want to use red roses for the altar arrangement in the sanctuary and also for the casket spray. They agreed enthusiastically, and I added, "Here's something to think about: After we finish the service at the cemetery, since she loved roses so much, you might want to take some long-stemmed roses out of the casket spray and then give one to each member of the family as a keepsake, as a remembrance of your mother. Just do it right there at the gravesite. It could be a very beautiful moment for your family."

Now, all the time we had been talking (I had been there with them for an hour or so), everybody was so tuned in, so focused on what we were doing. Everybody, that is, except little William, the eight-year-old grandson. He was sitting beside me on the couch, kicking his legs, fidgeting and yawning, and obviously feeling very uncomfortable with the whole thing. He never said a word. He just sat there doing what any normal eight-year-old boy would do in that situation—enduring it the best he could but wishing like everything he could get up and get out of there. I thought to myself, "Bless his heart. He isn't interested in any of this, and who could blame him. He's only eight years old. He is bored to tears, and he is certainly not paying attention at all."

Two days later at the cemetery, I found out how wrong

I was. The service at the church had gone beautifully. Then we went out to the cemetery. When we finished the brief committal service at the gravesite, I spoke to the family and hugged them all as they sat in those folding chairs under the green tent. Then I stepped out from under the tent and stood just outside, under a tree, to give the family their private moment there. The son and his wife stood and asked all the family members to remain seated so they could give each of them a red rose from the casket spray. It was a touching moment as each family member received a rose, but nothing could have prepared me for what happened next.

Little William got out of his seat and walked up to the casket. I wondered, *What on earth is he going to do?* His parents looked at him with a quizzical *What on earth is he going to do?* look as well. He stood on his tiptoes, reached up, pulled out a beautiful long-stemmed red rose, and walked over to me. He motioned for me to bend down so he could whisper something in my ear. I did, and he whispered, "I want you to have one." He handed me the rose. He hugged me tightly and then ran back under the tent and took his seat. It was a beautiful moment. I stood there with a rose in my hand and tears in my eyes. You see, I didn't think William had been listening, and yet he got the message better than anybody (including his pastor). With that simple, thoughtful gesture, he had said: "You're a member of our family, too," and he had brought me into the circle of love.

William is all grown up now. He has finished college and is working on his law degree at the University of Texas Law School. I hope he is still doing that. I hope he is still reaching out to bring others into the circle of love. Where did he learn that? He learned it from his grandmother and his parents and his church, but he learned it best from Jesus, who said, "Love one another as I have loved you," and who taught us over and over that life is worth living and people are worth loving.

THIRD AND FINALLY, CHRIST IS WORTH FOLLOWING

Do you want a great formula for living? Then remember Jesus Christ. Follow him. Imitate him. Learn from him. Serve him. Trust him.

Some years ago, a fire broke out in a hotel in Chicago. Flames and smoke blocked the normal escape routes. Some people on the tenth floor went out on a balcony to escape the smoke, but they were trapped there. It looked as if they were doomed. However, one man in the group braved the smoke and went back into the building. Fortunately, he found an exit to a fire escape. Courageously, he made his way back through the smoke and flames and led the group to safety. Another person in the group later said, "You can't imagine the feeling of relief and joy we felt when that man came back for us and said, 'This way out! Follow me! I know the way!' "

This is what the Christian gospel says to us: "Here is the One who knows the way to safety and life! Here is the One who can deliver you! Here is the One who can save you! Follow him, and you can live." Now, there is a sad footnote to this story about the Chicago hotel fire that serves as a parable for us. When the man came back to save the people, some of them followed his lead, but some refused to go with him! They didn't believe him. They didn't trust him. They didn't follow him. They gave up. They "sat on their ticket" and stayed on the balcony, and eventually they died. Life was there for them. Their ticket to safety was there. But they refused to accept it, and they perished.

Don't let that happen to you. Say yes to life, yes to other people, and yes to Christ. Minnie Louise Haskins, in "The Gate of the Year," said it powerfully:

> I said to the man who stood at the gate of the year, "Give me light that I may tread safely into the unknown." And he replied, "Go out into the darkness, and put your hand into the Hand of God. That shall be to you better than light and safer than a known way!"
>
> So, I went forth, and finding the Hand of God, trod gladly into the night.

Life is worth living, people are worth loving, and Christ is worth following.

SUGGESTIONS FOR LEADING A STUDY OF

If God Has a Refrigerator, Your Picture Is on It

JOHN D. SCHROEDER

This book by James W. Moore is a celebration of God's love for us and offers insights on how we can respond and nurture our relationship with God. As a leader, you have the opportunity to help members of your group become more effective Christians. Here are some suggestions to keep in mind as you begin:

1. You should review the entire book before your first group meeting so that you have an overview of the book and can be a better guide for the members of your group. You may want to use a highlighter to designate important points in the text.

2. Give a copy of the book to each participant before the first session and ask participants to read the introduction before your initial meeting. You may wish to limit the size of your group to ensure that everyone gets a chance to participate. Not everyone may feel comfortable reading aloud, answering questions, or participating

143

in group discussion or activities. Let group members know that this is okay, and encourage them to participate as they feel comfortable doing so.

3. Begin each session by reviewing the main points using the chapter summary. You may ask group members what they saw as highlights. Use your own reading, any notes you have taken, and this study guide to suggest other main points.

4. Select the discussion questions and activities you plan to use in advance. Use those you think will work best with your group. You may want to ask questions in a different order from the way they are presented in the study guide. Allow a reasonable amount of time for questions and a reasonable amount of time for one or two activities. You may create your own questions and activities if you desire.

5. Before moving from questions to activities, ask members if they have any questions that have not been answered.

6. Following the conclusion of the final activity, close with a short prayer. If your group desires, pause for individual prayer requests.

7. Start your meetings on time and try to end them on schedule.

8. If you ask a question and no one volunteers an answer, begin the discussion by suggesting an answer yourself. Then ask for comments and other answers.

9. Encourage total participation by asking questions of specific members. Your role is to give everyone who desires it the opportunity to talk and to be involved. Remember, you can always ask the questions "Why?" and "Can you explain in more detail?" to continue and deepen a discussion.

10. Be thankful and supportive. Thank members for their ideas and participation.

Introduction: If God Has a Refrigerator, Your Picture Is on It

CHAPTER SUMMARY

1. God is like the loving father in the prodigal son parable.
2. God loves us unconditionally.
3. God forgives us unreservedly.
4. God celebrates us unashamedly.

REFLECTION / DISCUSSION QUESTIONS

1. What new insights did you receive from reading this chapter?
2. In your own words, explain the meaning of the title of this book.
3. In your experience, in what ways has God been like a loving parent?
4. Why do people post things on their refrigerator?
5. What people or things figure prominently in your life, and why?
6. What examples of sacrificial and gracious love do you see in the story of Kurt Warner and his family?
7. Explain what it means to love unconditionally.
8. Give an example of a time when someone showed unconditional love to you.
9. How do we know that God always forgives us unreservedly?
10. Name someone whose parenting skills you admire, and explain how those skills are evident.
11. What does it mean that God celebrates us unashamedly?
12. Share a time when you celebrated something or someone unashamedly.

PRACTICAL APPLICATIONS / ACTIVITIES

1. In light of your reading of the introduction, reflect on / discuss your expectations as you begin this book.
2. Practice an act of unconditional love this week.
3. Celebrate the life of someone close to you.
4. Create a photo or art gallery on your refrigerator that illustrates God's love.
5. Make a list of some of your sins. Then, as a sign of God's forgiveness, destroy the list.

Prayer: *Dear God, thank you for remembering, cherishing, and loving us as your children. Forgive our foolish ways, and help us grow into mature Christians. Bless us and be with us as we learn more about you and ourselves. Amen.*

Chapter 1
Celebrating God's Beautiful Mind

CHAPTER SUMMARY

1. Our calling is to take on the mind of Christ.
2. Christlike humility is a trait of Christ's followers.
3. Christians are known by their obedience to God.
4. Christ's followers are known by their love.

REFLECTION / DISCUSSION QUESTIONS

1. What new insights did you receive from reading this chapter?
2. What does it mean to take on the mind of Christ?
3. In Philippians 2, how does the apostle Paul describe the mind of Christ?
4. Explain what *humility* means to you. Give an example.
5. How did God model humility for us?
6. What is meant by "Christlike obedience"?

7. What obstacles to obedience do we face today?

8. How did Christ model obedience?

9. What's the most challenging part of Christian obedience for you?

10. In what ways did Jesus model the meaning of love for us?

11. In your own words, explain the meaning of sacrificial love.

12. Recall a time when you were the recipient of sacrificial love.

PRACTICAL APPLICATIONS / ACTIVITIES

1. List some ways we can imitate the sacrificial love of Christ.

2. Reflect on / discuss: What shapes our mind in Christlike ways? in ways that are not Christlike?

3. Provide biblical examples of Christlike humility, obedience, and love.

4. Spend time in prayer this week asking God to help you be more Christlike.

5. Reflect on / discuss which people and experiences have taught you about Christlike humility, obedience, and love.

Prayer: *Dear God, we thank you for Christ's example of how to be obedient, how to be humble, and how to love others. Help us to be more Christlike. May we accept your call to reach out to others and to be your heart, hands, and voice in our world. Amen.*

Chapter 2
Celebrating God's Strength

CHAPTER SUMMARY

1. Encouragement means to be full of heart.
2. Endurance means to be full of power.
3. Enthusiasm means to be full of God.
4. God gives us strength to meet any foe.

REFLECTION / DISCUSSION QUESTIONS

1. What new insights did you receive from reading this chapter?
2. Explain what encouragement means to you.
3. Give some biblical examples of God providing encouragement.
4. Recall a time when you needed and were given encouragement.
5. What does it mean to have endurance? Give a biblical example.
6. What gives you endurance?
7. Share a time in your life when your endurance made the difference.
8. Explain what having enthusiasm means to you. What triggers enthusiasm?
9. Give an example of someone you know who has enthusiasm.
10. Share a time when enthusiasm gave you the lift you needed.
11. What do we need in order to obtain encouragement, endurance, and enthusiasm? Do these come from God, from within, or both?
12. Reflect on / discuss examples of God's strength that you have observed in your church, in your community, or in the world.

PRACTICAL APPLICATIONS / ACTIVITIES

1. "God gives us strength." Discuss what this means.
2. Offer encouragement to someone this week.
3. Talk with a friend or family member this week about "the 3 Es"—encouragement, endurance, and enthusiasm.
4. Start a project or set a goal, and use your God-given endurance to see it through.
5. Talk about / reflect on the importance of the 3 Es in relation to coping with a major disappointment or hardship.

Prayer: *Dear God, you give us strength to face any foe. Grant us your gifts of encouragement, enthusiasm, and endurance, so that we may fight the good fight. Help us use our talents to serve others. Be with us this coming week. Amen.*

Chapter 3
Celebrating God's Urgent Priorities

CHAPTER SUMMARY

1. Don't put off saying "I'm sorry" to someone.
2. If you need to say "I love you", do it now.
3. Say "yes" to God. Don't wait.
4. Life is too short and too fragile. Do it now.

REFLECTION / DISCUSSION QUESTIONS

1. What new insights did you receive from reading this chapter?
2. From your reading of the Scripture and this chapter, what did Paul ask of Timothy, and why did he ask it? How do you think Timothy responded?

3. What causes us to put things off? List some of the most common reasons.

4. Have you ever put something off until it was too late? Explain.

5. Share a time when it was important that someone said "I'm sorry" to you or you said "I'm sorry" to someone else.

6. Why is it so important to say you are sorry? Who benefits, and why?

7. Why do we often neglect to say we love someone?

8. What causes us to be reluctant to say "yes" to God?

9. How do you decide whether or not something is a priority? Give some guidelines.

10. How do you fight procrastination? What advice would you give to someone who has a chronic problem with this?

11. What are some common consequences of delay?

12. How do you know when God is calling you or asking you to do something?

PRACTICAL APPLICATIONS / ACTIVITIES

1. Talk about steps needed to fix broken relationships.

2. List your urgent priorities and contrast them with God's urgent priorities.

3. Discuss the "come before winter" story, as the author describes it.

4. Find examples in the Bible of lost opportunities, and reflect on or discuss how things might have turned out differently in each example.

5. Reflect this week on what God wants you to do. Take some action.

Prayer: *Dear God, we celebrate that our care and welfare are your urgent priorities. Move us to avoid procrastination* and to share with others the important messages of life. Help us say "yes" to you and to your will for our lives. In all circumstances, may we continue to look to you for guidance. Amen.

Chapter 4
Celebrating God's Unconditional Love

CHAPTER SUMMARY

1. God loves and accepts us just the way we are.
2. Unconditional love is the answer for our family relationships.
3. Unconditional love is the answer for our relationships with others.
4. Unconditional love is the answer for our relationship with God.

REFLECTION / DISCUSSION QUESTIONS

1. What new insights did you receive from reading this chapter?
2. In your own words, explain what it means to love unconditionally.
3. Talk about someone who loves you unconditionally, or describe an example of unconditional love you have observed.
4. Explain why unconditional love is the real test of faith.
5. What sometimes prevents us from practicing unconditional love?
6. Talk about someone you love unconditionally.
7. How do we benefit when we practice unconditional love?
8. Explain how unconditional love can strengthen family relationships.

9. What is needed to practice unconditional love with others?

10. How and why do we sometimes put conditions on our love for God?

11. How can we become more loving?

12. Why does practicing unconditional love involve risk?

PRACTICAL APPLICATIONS / ACTIVITIES

1. List ways we can celebrate God's unconditional love.

2. Find and reflect on / discuss biblical examples of unconditional love.

3. Talk about unconditional love with a friend or family member.

4. Identify and reflect on / discuss examples of unconditional love from newspapers or periodicals.

5. Practice unconditional love this week.

Prayer: *Dear God, thank you for loving and accepting us just as we are. Help us practice unconditional love in our relationships with family and others. We pray that our love may be a healing force and will bring us closer together with others. Be with us as we continue to celebrate the many blessings we receive from you. Amen.*

Chapter 5
Celebrating God's Key to Real Life

CHAPTER SUMMARY

1. The key to life is to seek God's will.

2. A second key to life is to obey God's Word.

3. A third key to life is to strive to live a life pleasing to God.

4. Our chief purpose is to celebrate God, to serve, and to enjoy God forever.

REFLECTION / DISCUSSION QUESTIONS

1. What new insights did you receive from reading this chapter?

2. What is meant by the sentence "If God is your co-pilot, swap seats"?

3. What prevents us from making God our chief pilot?

4. List some things the world wants us to believe are keys to life.

5. How do we seek the will of God? How do we know if we are doing God's will?

6. How is trust involved in our relationship with God?

7. How is God's perspective different from our own perspective?

8. Why, according to the author, is the Bible so important for us?

9. What guidelines should we have for making daily decisions?

10. Recall a time when you struggled to know God's will. How did you deal with your struggle?

11. How are *seeking, obeying,* and *living* God's will tied together?

12. What does it mean to "live God's way"?

PRACTICAL APPLICATIONS / ACTIVITIES

1. Talk with others to learn how people discern God's will for their lives.

2. List ways we find joy, meaning, and mission in life.

3. Make a list of things you'd like to talk to God about.

4. Conduct a survey regarding what people believe are the keys to real life.

5. Reflect and pray about seeking God's will, obeying God's Word, and living God's way.

Prayer: *Dear God, thank you for giving us the keys to real life. Help us seek your will, obey your word, and walk in your ways. May we reach out in love to others, and may we learn what it means to forgive and forget. Be with us as we often struggle to do what is right. Amen.*

Chapter 6
Celebrating God's Enduring Music

CHAPTER SUMMARY

1. Keep on celebrating life, no matter what life brings.
2. Turn disappointments into instruments of victory.
3. Turn heartaches into instruments of victory.
4. Turn sorrows into instruments of victory.

REFLECTION / DISCUSSION QUESTIONS

1. What new insights did you receive from reading this chapter?
2. Explain the meaning of "making music with what we have left."
3. Recall a disappointment and how you dealt with it.
4. How did you deal with disappointment as a child? Contrast that with how you deal with disappointment as an adult.
5. How does God want us to deal with disappointments in life?
6. What is the message of Matthew 25 and the calling of every Christian?
7. Explain what a painful heartache is, and give an example.
8. What do you think the difference is between heartache and sorrow?
9. What sorrows and heartaches have crossed your path, and how have you dealt with them?

10. What resources does God give us to handle life's challenges?

11. Who has been an inspiration to you in dealing with disappointment, sorrow, or heartache, and in what ways?

12. What are the benefits when we tackle and triumph over adversity?

PRACTICAL APPLICATIONS / ACTIVITIES

1. Locate promises in the Bible on which we can lean in times of trouble.

2. Brainstorm some strategies for turning around a bad situation.

3. Reflect on / discuss incidents and reactions to sorrow and disappointment as found in the Bible.

4. List some ways you can help someone who is experiencing disappointment, sorrow, or heartache.

5. Share what you learned from this lesson with a friend or family member.

Prayer: *Dear God, we thank you that you are with us in both good times and difficult times. Help us celebrate your presence and always look to you for guidance. Thank you for being with us always and for your blessings. Amen.*

Chapter 7
Celebrating God's Greatest Promise

CHAPTER SUMMARY

1. God is always with us.
2. We find Jesus Christ wherever people are in worship.
3. We find Jesus Christ wherever people are serving.
4. We find Jesus Christ wherever people are suffering.

REFLECTION / DISCUSSION QUESTIONS

1. What new insights did you receive from reading this chapter?

2. When someone makes a promise to you, what are your expectations?

3. Where do you go to find God and to feel the presence of God?

4. What does it mean to you personally to know that "God is with you always"?

5. Recall a time when you felt especially close to God.

6. The author says that the best place to glimpse the Risen Christ is in your church; explain why this may be so.

7. What do you enjoy most about worshiping God in church?

8. God puts us to work serving others. How does this influence our faith and the faith of others?

9. In what ways do you feel called to serve God?

10. How easy or how hard is it for you to "go out to the world" to serve others? Explain.

11. Why do people often feel God so vividly when they are suffering?

12. In what ways is God like a loving parent?

PRACTICAL APPLICATIONS / ACTIVITIES

1. Discuss how suffering can be beneficial to us.

2. Search the Bible for promises made about God's presence.

3. Share with a friend or family member something you learned from this chapter.

4. Perform an act of kindness for a stranger this week.

5. Carry a reminder with you this week that God is with you every moment of each day.

Prayer: *Dear God, we thank you for your promise that we can depend on you at all times and in all situations. You are always there when we need you, whether we realize it or not. Help us reach out to others so that we truly may be your servants. Amen.*

Chapter 8
Celebrating God's Healing Love

CHAPTER SUMMARY

1. There is nothing more powerful than the healing power of love.
2. Love can heal us physically.
3. Love can heal us emotionally.
4. Love can heal us spiritually.

REFLECTION / DISCUSSION QUESTIONS

1. What new insights did you receive from reading this chapter?
2. Recall a time when love healed you.
3. What do we need to do in order to be healed by love?
4. What does God want us to do with the gift of love we are given?
5. What is known about the power of love to heal physically?
6. What kinds of "people skills" are important for a physician, and how do these skills relate to love?
7. What is the difference between emotional and physical healing?
8. How has God's love made a difference in your life?
9. List some types and examples of emotional healing.
10. Who can perform spiritual healing? What is needed to do so?

11. How do you know when you've been spiritually healed?

12. What makes love so powerful?

PRACTICAL APPLICATIONS / ACTIVITIES

1. Look for biblical examples of the power of love.

2. From your observations in your life, in your community, or in the world, create a list of examples of the healing power of love.

3. Write a brief essay about the role that love has played in your life, or use paper and crayons to illustrate God's healing love.

4. Talk with a family member or friend about God's healing love. If you are comfortable doing so, reflect on and share with each other the kind of healing each of you most needs at this time—physical, emotional, or spiritual. Talk about ways to encourage and help each other bring about that kind of healing in your lives.

5. Pray each day, asking God to bring healing to your life and to the lives of others.

Prayer: *Dear God, we thank you for the love that heals and connects us to you and to others. Help us put love into practice each day so that we become your instruments of healing. Show us how to overcome the ills that threaten us. May we remember that you are with us always. Amen.*

Chapter 9
Celebrating God's Call to Discipleship

CHAPTER SUMMARY

1. God offers us forgiveness and a new start.

2. Jesus calls us to a new direction.

3. Jesus can give us a new future.
4. Jesus calls us to live a new lifestyle.

REFLECTION / DISCUSSION QUESTIONS

1. What new insights did you receive from reading this chapter?
2. When you think of discipleship, what comes to mind?
3. What does Jesus want when he calls us to follow him?
4. Explain what it means to practice discipleship.
5. How does God equip us for discipleship?
6. Reflect on / talk about a time when you have felt "lost," without direction or purpose.
7. Share what gives you a sense of direction and a sense of purpose.
8. How does God offer us a sense of direction?
9. Why is Jesus more interested in our future than in our past?
10. Part of Jesus' message, the author says, is that in order to be a follower, you must "deny yourself." In your own words, what do you think this means?
11. What kind of new lifestyle does God desire for us?
12. How is your life changed when you decide to follow Jesus?

PRACTICAL APPLICATIONS / ACTIVITIES

1. List the costs and benefits of following Jesus.
2. Find examples in the Bible of Jesus' promises to his followers.
3. Use your Bible to identify those who accepted Jesus' call to "follow me," and discuss how their lives were changed as followers.
4. Survey friends and family about discipleship and its meaning.

5. Reflect on and pray this week about what Jesus wants from you as a disciple.

Prayer: *Jesus, you call us to follow you. We try, but sometimes we fall short. Help us to be the disciples you know we can be. Thank you for all the love and support you provide. Bless us on our journey as your disciples. Amen.*

Chapter 10
Celebrating God's Three Ways of Acting

CHAPTER SUMMARY

1. We sing praise to the Father-Creator.
2. We sing praise to the Son-Savior.
3. We sing praise to the Holy Spirit-Sustainer.
4. Don't get lost in questions; just join in the song!

REFLECTION / DISCUSSION QUESTIONS

1. What new insights did you receive from reading this chapter?
2. At what stage in your faith did you begin to be aware of the concept of the Trinity—"one God in three persons"?
3. How is the doctrine of the Trinity like the concept of love?
4. What does it mean to us that God is the Father-Creator?
5. Reflect on / discuss why God created us and this world.
6. What does it mean to us that God is the Son-Savior?
7. What does it mean to have a *personal* relationship with Jesus Christ?
8. Reflect on / discuss this statement: "God's incredible love not only *makes* us; it also *saves* us."

9. What does it mean to us that God is the Holy Spirit-Sustainer?

10. Share how God has sustained you in tough times.

11. Explain what is meant by the statement "Every belief was first a song."

12. For you, personally, what are the most fulfilling ways in which you relate to, celebrate, and praise God?

PRACTICAL APPLICATIONS / ACTIVITIES

1. Examine the Bible to discover what it says about the Trinity—God the Father, God the Son, and God the Holy Spirit.

2. Reflect upon and compare the three ways in which people experience or relate to God through the Trinity.

3. Share with a family member or friend one insight you gained from this lesson.

4. Make a list of things that we just accept by faith.

5. Use a hymnal or songbook to locate songs of praise relating to the Trinity, and reflect on the meaning of the words.

Prayer: *Dear God, we experience you as our Creator, Savior, and Sustainer. We thank you for your continuing involvement in our lives. Make us open to your guiding. Bless us and be with us during the coming week. Amen.*

Chapter 11
Celebrating God's Gift of the Church

CHAPTER SUMMARY

1. The church recharges our spiritual batteries.

2. The church reminds us of how much God loves us.

3. The church reminds us of the importance of practicing the holy habits.

4. The church reminds us of the power of Jesus.

REFLECTION / DISCUSSION QUESTIONS

1. What new insights did you receive from reading this chapter?
2. Share why you are involved in church activities.
3. Share some early memories of attending church.
4. God has given us the church. What does God expect from us in return?
5. What's your favorite part of a church service, and why?
6. Explain the benefits of going to church on a regular basis.
7. What happens when our spiritual batteries run low?
8. In what ways is God's love evident in church?
9. List some holy habits and how they contribute to spiritual health.
10. Recall a time when you needed a spiritual recharge and how the church helped you.
11. How are we reminded of the power of Jesus each Sunday in church?
12. What do you personally miss most when you are unable to attend church?

PRACTICAL APPLICATIONS / ACTIVITIES

1. List some strategies for getting the most benefit from belonging to a church.
2. Survey fellow church members to learn what people find most fulfilling about being involved in church.
3. Create a list of ministry opportunities within the church.
4. Brainstorm ideas of gifts that you can give to your church. Select one gift and give it to your church during the coming week.
5. Invite someone to attend church with you this week.

Prayer: *Dear God, we thank you for your gift of the church and for all it means to us. Help us cherish it and not take it for granted. Open our eyes to the many possibilities for service and spiritual growth. Bless our pastors, our leaders, and those who teach others about you and your love. Amen.*

Chapter 12
Celebrating God's Gift of Freedom

CHAPTER SUMMARY

1. Self-pity can imprison us.
2. Resentment can imprison us.
3. The rush to success can imprison us.
4. God sets us free from all our prisons.

REFLECTION / DISCUSSION QUESTIONS

1. What new insights did you receive from reading this chapter?
2. How does the world "squeeze us into its mold"? Give some examples.
3. What are the dangers of self-pity?
4. Recall a time you were imprisoned by self-pity.
5. Reflect on / discuss some ideas for breaking free from self-pity.
6. What is meant by the statement "God made us for the skies"?
7. Why is resentment a prison? How does it harm us?
8. Recall a past resentment and how it affected you.
9. Reflect on /discuss strategies for breaking free of resentment.
10. What does it mean to be a success? How does the world's view of success compare and contrast with the Bible's view of success?

11. Why is "the rush to success" a prison for so many people?

12. Reflect on / discuss biblical examples of how Jesus set free persons who were imprisoned.

PRACTICAL APPLICATIONS / ACTIVITIES

1. See how many examples of "prisons" you can find in a daily newspaper.

2. List some warning signs that we may be putting ourselves in a prison, as well as reasons why it is easier to get into a prison than to break free from it.

3. Create a list of all the freedoms that God has given us.

4. Reflect on ways we can celebrate our freedoms.

5. Reread Romans 12:1-2. Talk to God in prayer, asking God to transform you by the renewing of your mind. Reflect on God's will for your life.

Prayer: *Dear God, we are thankful for the many freedoms you give us. Help us not to take them for granted. Open the eyes of people everywhere, so that the world may see that you are the answer to our longings. In Jesus' name. Amen.*

Chapter 13
Celebrating the Spirit of Christ

CHAPTER SUMMARY

1. Living in the spirit of Christ, we see people to help.

2. Living in the spirit of Christ, we see problems to solve.

3. Living in the spirit of Christ, we see opportunities to serve.

4. Put your trust in the spirit of Christ.

Study Guide

REFLECTION / DISCUSSION QUESTIONS

1. What new insights did you receive from reading this chapter?
2. Recall a time when you put your trust in the wrong place or the wrong person.
3. Name some people you trust, and explain why you trust them.
4. What happens when you look at life through the eyes of Christ?
5. In your own words, explain what it means to live in the spirit of Christ.
6. What causes us sometimes not to see people who need help?
7. Recall a time when you saw someone in need and provided help.
8. How can God help you see and solve problems?
9. How does God want us to react to opportunities to serve?
10. Recall a time you accepted an opportunity to serve, and share how you benefited from the experience.
11. Reread John 13:34-35. How does Jesus say we are to love one another? What does he mean by this?
12. Who are some of the people you know who need help right now? What can you do to offer and provide that help?

PRACTICAL APPLICATIONS / ACTIVITIES

1. From your own life, make a list of examples of how you place your trust in others, and how others place their trust in you.
2. Make a list of opportunities for service and for problem solving.
3. Find biblical illustrations of trust.

4. Talk with a friend or family member about trust.

5. Reflect upon your trust in God. Pray about trust, asking God for the strength to trust, and to be worthy of the trust others place in you.

Prayer: *Dear God, thank you for your love and for all you do for us. Help us trust you and look to you for answers to the challenges we face. Guide our words and actions so that they may be used by you to further your Kingdom. Amen.*

Chapter 14

Celebrating God's Blueprint for Life

CHAPTER SUMMARY

1. Life is worth living.
2. People are worth loving.
3. Christ is worth following.
4. Life is God's gift to us.

REFLECTION / DISCUSSION QUESTIONS

1. What new insights did you receive from reading this chapter?

2. What do you think the apostle Paul meant in Philippians 2:12 when he said, "Work out your own salvation with fear and trembling; for it is God who is at work in you"?

3. List reasons why life is worth living.

4. Where do we look to find God's blueprint for our life?

5. What does God want us to do with the gift of life?

6. Recall a day when life felt worth living and a day when it did not.

7. Explain why people are worth loving.

8. Name some people you love and explain why you love them.

9. Reflect on / discuss: If you could instantly change your life, how would you change it?

10. How would you tell someone that Christ is worth following?

11. Name a lesson about life that you learned as a child.

12. Explain this statement: What we do with our life is our gift to God.

PRACTICAL APPLICATIONS / ACTIVITIES

1. Reflect on / discuss: Which chapter in this book had the greatest impact on you? Explain.

2. Share with a friend or family member some things you learned from reading this book.

3. Compile a list of some of the choices that people face each day.

4. Create your own formula for living—your own personal mission statement.

5. Make a personal commitment, supported by prayer, to be a living example of God's unconditional love.

Prayer: *Dear God, we thank you for your gift of life. Thank you for being in relationship with us and for letting us know in so many ways just how important each one of us is to you. Help us this week and always to follow the path of Jesus Christ in our spiritual walk with you, trusting in your word as revealed to us in the Bible. May we show love to all as we seek to serve others in your name. And may we always remember that our picture is on your refrigerator. Amen.*